About Family...

Name: Sophia

Sophia is my best sister who always be kind to me always not even once she bees mean to me.

Name: Mamita

Mamita is my grama who lives in colombia but she goes to miami to take care of us also she only speaks spanish.

Name: Sarah

Sarah is my big sister
who loves me so much.
She live in Daytona.

Name: tia

tia will have two
babies one will be a
boy and one will be
a girl.

FLORIDA

Treasures

A Reading/Language Arts Program

Mc Graw Hill **Macmillan/McGraw-Hill**

Contributors

Time Magazine, Accelerated Reader

learning through listening

Students with print disabilities may be eligible to obtain an accessible, audio version of the pupil edition of this textbook. Please call Recording for the Blind & Dyslexic at 1-800-221-4792 for complete information.

B

The McGraw·Hill Companies

Macmillan McGraw-Hill

Published by Macmillan/McGraw-Hill, of McGraw-Hill Education, a division of The McGraw-Hill Companies, Inc., Two Penn Plaza, New York, New York 10121.

Printed in the United States of America

ISBN-13: 978-0-02-198763-4/2, Bk. 2

ISBN-10: 0-02-198763-7/2, Bk. 2

2 3 4 5 6 7 8 9 (058/034) 11 10 09 08

FLORIDA
Treasures

A Reading/Language Arts Program

Program Authors

Dr. Donald R. Bear
University of Nevada, Reno
Reno, Nevada

Dr. Janice A. Dole
University of Utah
Salt Lake City, Utah

Dr. Douglas Fisher
San Diego State University
San Diego, California

Dr. Vicki Gibson
Longmire Learning Center, Inc.
College Station, Texas

Dr. Jana Echevarria
California State University, Long Beach
Long Beach, California

Dr. Jan E. Hasbrouck
Educational Consultant - J.H. Consulting
Seattle, Washington

Dr. Scott G. Paris
University of Michigan
Ann Arbor, Michigan

Dr. Timothy Shanahan
University of Illinois at Chicago
Chicago, Illinois

Dr. Josefina V. Tinajero
University of Texas at El Paso
El Paso, Texas

Macmillan/McGraw-Hill

Unit 4

Land, Sea, Sky

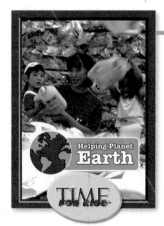

5

Unit 5

Discoveries

Award
Winning
Selection

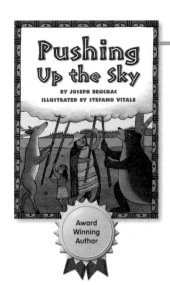

Award
Winning
Author

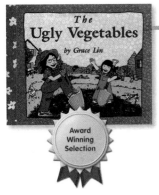

Unit 6 Expressions

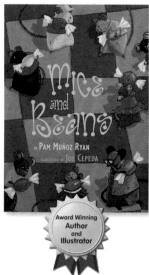

Award Winning Author and Illustrator

Award Winning Author

FCAT

Talk About It

What do animals and humans need to live?

LOG ON Find out more about animal needs at
www.macmillanmh.com

Animal Needs

Animals Need to Eat

by Patty Serrano

All animals need to eat, but different **beasts** eat in different ways.

A raccoon searches for fish, nuts, and other things to eat. Raccoons wash all their food before eating it. To do this, they must live near water. Even small pools of water, like **puddles**, will do. After the raccoon washes its food, it begins to eat by taking small bites. The animal may **nibble** on an acorn once it is clean.

A tiger hunts for the meat it eats. Eating can make a mess out of the tiger's fur. There are many places that need to be scratched. To get rid of these **itches**, the tiger bathes in a pond. Later the tiger may lie in the sun and **preen**. It carefully smooths its fur with its tongue.

A spider eats meat, too. It builds a sticky web and then hides. The web is a useful tool for the spider. Bugs get stuck in the **handy** web. Then the spider's dinner can't escape.

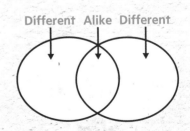

Reread for **Comprehension**

Ask Questions

FCAT Compare and Contrast

Asking questions can help you **compare and contrast** parts of an article. To compare means to tell how things are alike. To contrast means to tell how they are different. Reread to find out how animals get food and to compare and contrast the animals in the selection.

Different Alike Different

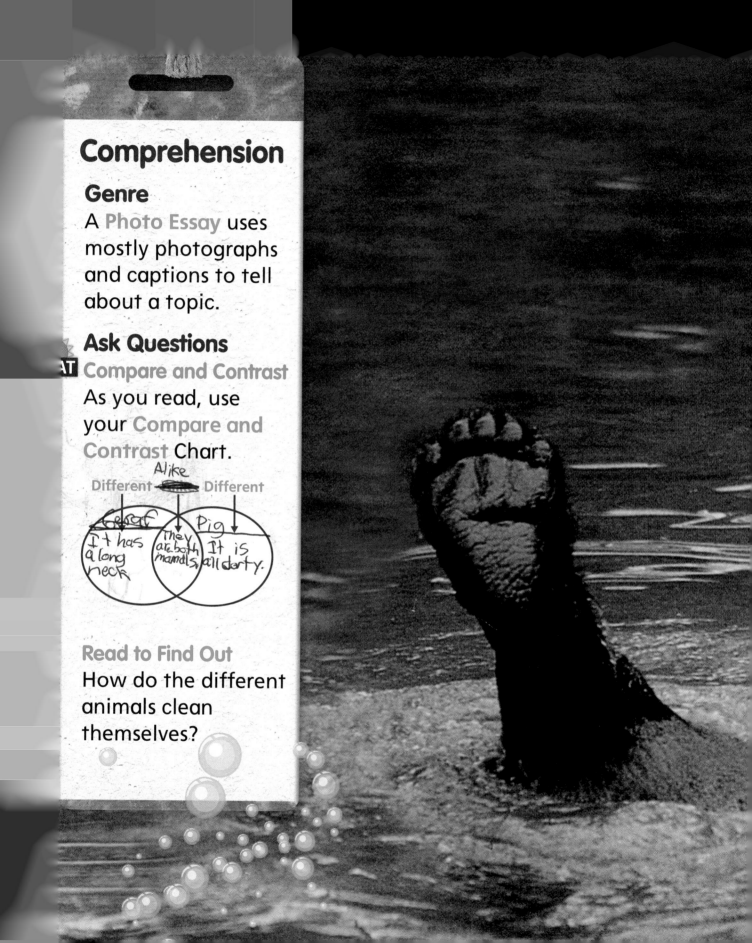

Comprehension

Genre
A **Photo Essay** uses mostly photographs and captions to tell about a topic.

Ask Questions
Compare and Contrast As you read, use your **Compare and Contrast** Chart.

Alike
Different — Different

It has a long neck
They are both mamals
Pig It is all dirty.

Read to Find Out
How do the different animals clean themselves?

Splish!
Splash!
ANIMAL BATHS

Award
Winning
Author

by APRIL PULLEY SAYRE

SPLISH! SPLASH!

Take a bath.

Brush your
teeth clean.

And think of
the animals.

They clean
themselves, too.

Squirt!

An elephant sprays
water over its back.

Squirt!!

Baby will get a
shower, too.

16

Pigs take their baths in thick, brown mud. They soak, slog, snort...and seem to smile. Mud cools their skin. And best of all, it gets rid of **itches**, as well.

Birds take baths in **puddles**. Or shower under sprinklers or waterfalls.

Once clean, they **preen**—
smoothing, fluffing, and
straightening their feathers.
That's like hair brushing for you.

 FCAT Compare and Contrast
What do birds do after
bathing that pigs do not?

Ducks do extra work. They spread oil on their feathers. This special oil waterproofs them. Without it, ducks would get soggy and cold... which wouldn't be *ducky* at all!

Bears have long fur that gets itchy and full of insects.
To scratch itches, a bear rubs against a tree.
Bears also take dust baths. They roll in dirt.
Or they swim and splash in a wide, cool stream.

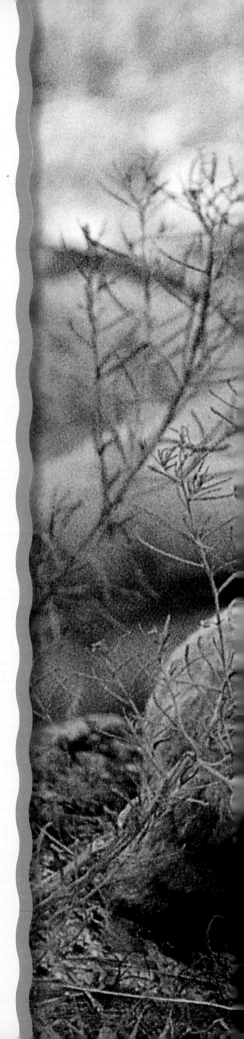

Even the king of **beasts** can get beastly dirty. So lions do what house cats do. They lick their long fur clean. But even a lion's tongue can't reach the back of its head... so it licks a paw and rubs it over its head and ears.

A comb might come in **handy** for cleaning a chimpanzee's fur. But chimps don't have combs, so fingers work fine.

Chimps bite and pull bugs and leaves
from their family's and friends' fur.
What are good buddies for?

Oxpeckers, a type of bird, spend their time hanging around. Where? On the bodies of giraffes. Giraffes don't seem to mind. Oxpeckers peck away ticks. They get a meal, and the giraffe gets clean.

Hippos have helpers, too. But these helpers are underwater, in the rivers and ponds where hippos wade. Fish **nibble** algae off a hippo's skin. Does it tickle the hippo? Only hippos know. And they won't say.

Fish don't take baths. They live in water. But some do try to stay clean. Big fish wait in line—not for a car wash, but for a cleaner fish.

Nibble, nibble, the cleaner fish bites tiny pests off the big fish's scales. The big fish gets clean. The cleaner fish gets a meal. Now that's an amazing deal!

FCAT Compare and Contrast
How do some animals use help from another animal to stay clean?

Nearby, a shrimp crawls into a moray eel's mouth.

Will it become a shrimp dinner? Not this time. It's a cleaner shrimp— an animal dentist.

It picks and eats food off the moray's teeth. Instead of being a shrimp dinner, it's dinnertime for this shrimp!

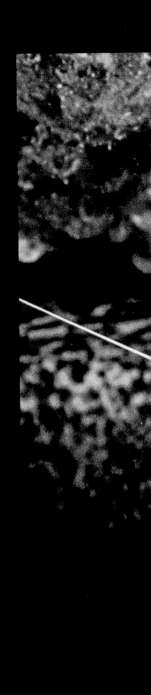

Now that you've heard
about animal baths and animal
dentists, and how animals splish,
splash, peck, and preen...
it's time to take *your* bath.

Splish and splash.

And think of the animals.
They, too, are getting clean.

Splish! Splash!
April Has Fun on the Job

April Pulley Sayre has written more than 50 books. Many of them are about plants and animals.

"As a child," April says, "I spent hours picking flowers, watching insects, reading books, and writing. Now I do the same thing, only as a career." April's favorite part of the work is researching. She likes reading books and magazines, calling people, and visiting museums, parks, and wild places.

Other books written by April Pulley Sayre

 Find out more about April Pulley Sayre at **www.macmillanmh.com**

FCAT Author's Purpose

The author explains how animals clean. Write a list of what you do to keep clean.

FCAT Comprehension Check

Retell the Story

Use the Retelling Cards to retell the selection.

Retelling Cards

Think and Compare

Different Alike Different

1. How are the animals alike in this selection? How are they different? Use information and details from the story to explain your answer. **Ask Questions: Compare and Contrast**

2. Reread pages 26–27. Why might a comb come in **handy** for a chimp? **Analyze**

3. Which animal do you think bathes in the most unusual way? Why? **Evaluate**

4. Why do animals need to keep clean? **Apply**

5. How is "Animals Need to Eat" on pages 12–13 like *Splish! Splash!* ? How is it different? **Reading/Writing Across Texts**

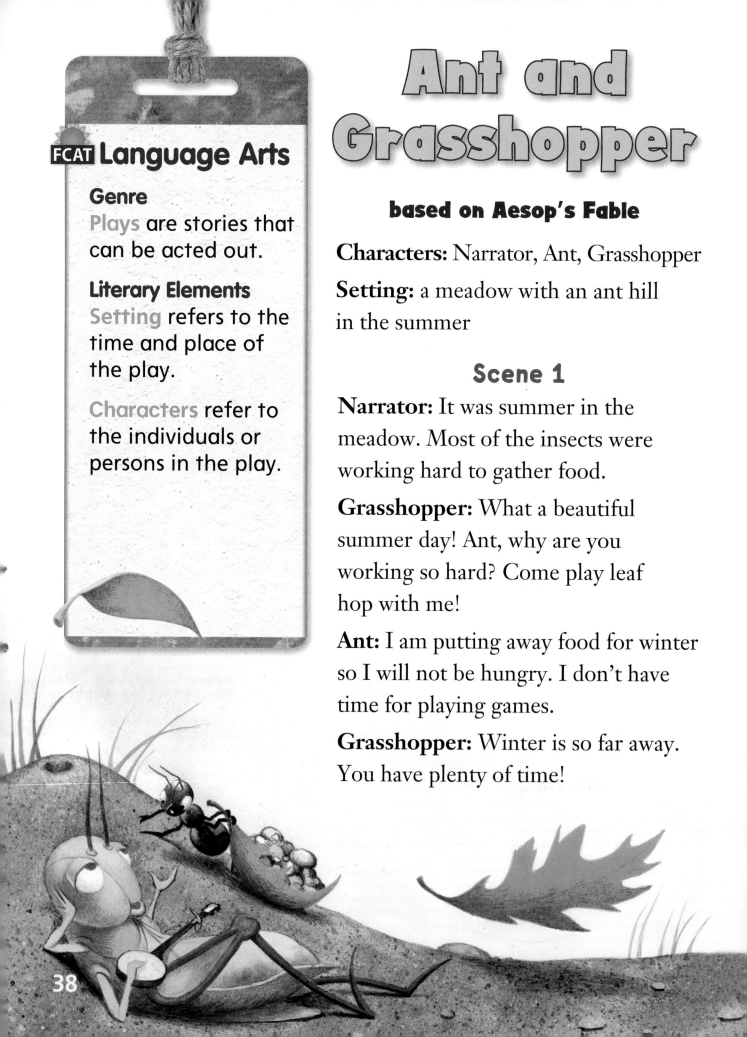

Ant and Grasshopper

based on Aesop's Fable

Characters: Narrator, Ant, Grasshopper

Setting: a meadow with an ant hill in the summer

Scene 1

Narrator: It was summer in the meadow. Most of the insects were working hard to gather food.

Grasshopper: What a beautiful summer day! Ant, why are you working so hard? Come play leaf hop with me!

Ant: I am putting away food for winter so I will not be hungry. I don't have time for playing games.

Grasshopper: Winter is so far away. You have plenty of time!

Ant: Winter lasts as long as summer. You have to be ready! I think you should save some food.

Grasshopper: I'll do it next week. There is no rush.

Narrator: Week after week, Ant worked. Week after week, Grasshopper played leaf hop.

Scene 2

Narrator: Soon winter came. The meadow was covered with snow. There was no food to be found.

Grasshopper: Ant, please help me. I am cold and hungry.

Ant: Oh Grasshopper, you did not plan. I will give you some food, but next summer you must gather food for yourself.

Narrator: Ant gave Grasshopper some food. Ant also taught Grasshopper an important lesson!

FCAT Connect and Compare

1. Why is the setting of the play important to the action? **Setting**

2. Think about the play and the story *Splish! Splash!* How do the animals in both selections meet their needs? **Reading/Writing Across Texts**

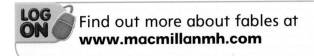

LOG ON Find out more about fables at
www.macmillanmh.com

FCAT Writer's Craft

Topic Sentence
Remember to write a good topic sentence for each paragraph. A good topic sentence tells what the paragraph is about.

② Notes

① Notes
Chimpanzees, Africa,

rocks
sticks

③ Notes
take leaves off the sticks, poke sticks in termite hill, eat insects off stick

The paragraph begins with a topic sentence.

This sentence supports my topic sentence.

Chimps Need Tools

by Jewel W.

Chimps need simple tools to get food. In Africa, they need to find rocks to crack open nuts. Chimps also need sticks to get and eat termites from termite hills.

Writing Prompt

All animals have needs.

Think about animals that you know about. Find out facts about their needs.

Now, write a summary about animal needs.

FCAT Writer's Checklist

✓ **Focus:** My writing is clearly about animal needs.

☐ **Organization:** My writing includes a good topic sentence.

✓ **Support:** I include details that support my topic sentence.

✓ **Conventions:** The punctuation in my sentences is correct.

Animal Survival

Talk About It

How do animals survive in the wild?

LOG ON Find out more about animal survival at **www.macmillanmh.com**

Bill Helps Geese Survive

by Anthony Estes

As a boy, Bill pictured himself flying. In his mind, he would **imagine** soaring through the sky with the birds. Bill never gave up his dream. He learned to fly airplanes.

One day, Bill found a nest of young geese. They were **deserted**. Their mother had gone away and left the babies. Bill took the geese home and cared for them.

Soon the geese learned to fly. A few had trouble with their **balance**. They would flop from side to side. At first, the geese only flew around Bill's yard.

Then, the geese flew over more land. When the geese learned to fly over a **wider** area, Bill decided they needed a safe place to live.

Fall was coming. The ground where Bill lives **freezes** early. Soon the ground would be too cold for the geese to live. Bill didn't want the geese to die. It would be the **saddest** thing to happen. Bill would feel very unhappy.

Bill decided to lead the geese south, where it is warmer. They could follow his plane. His plan worked. At last, Bill was able to fly with the birds.

Reread for **Comprehension**

Ask Questions

FCAT **Cause and Effect**

Asking questions is one way to figure out the **cause and effect** of events in an article. A cause is why something happens. An effect is what happens. Reread the article and use the chart to help you identify the cause and effect of events.

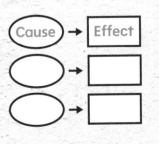

Comprehension

Genre
Realistic Fiction is a made-up story that could happen in real life.

Ask Questions
Cause and Effect
As you read, use your Cause and Effect Chart.

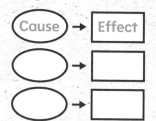

Read to Find Out
What happens to the goose and how does it affect her life?

46

Goose's Story

by Cari Best · illustrated by Holly Meade

Henry hears the honking first. He circles the pond, around and a half, sending up splashes of warm spring mud all over his winter coat. Henry knows the geese are coming. And then I know it, too.

They land in couples and stand in threes and band together in bunches like people. Old geese, young geese, grandmas, uncles, cousins, and nieces. Each one painted in black and white and gray and brown.

Some geese sit and some geese sleep. Some drink and bathe and swim and sun. Pecking and nibbling, they celebrate spring. All afternoon.

49

Then Henry breaks free to take back his pond. And the Sunday geese jump for the sky. Their wings spread **wider** than my arms can reach. Their legs tuck under like airplane wheels. There is honking and barking—and giggles from me.

50

Until I see her. One goose alone. She doesn't flutter her feathers or hiss at Henry. She doesn't stretch out her neck. And she doesn't fly away.

"Go!" I shout and stamp my boots. But the goose doesn't move.

She stares at us and we stare at her. First at what is right about her. And then at what is wrong.

"It's your foot!" I whisper. And then I can't move either.

My heart is thumping so loud I'm sure she can hear it. "Oh, goose," I say, "what happened to you?"

I want to stay and watch her. Make sure she's all right. But I might scare her even more. And I'm scared, too. So I lead Henry toward our house. To Mama and Papa inside.

The next day when I see the goose, her foot is gone.
I feel the **saddest** I've ever felt. I stand on one foot
myself, fixing my eyes on the geese at the other side
of the pond. Losing my **balance** when I've counted to
thirty-seven.

"Unlucky goose," says Papa, looking away.

"Some kind of accident," says Mama, looking angry.

FCAT Cause and Effect
Why do the girl's feelings
change about the goose?

For the rest of the spring, the other geese swim and the other geese nibble. They build their nests and show off their young. Soon they teach the babies to follow and the babies to swim. To stay away from raccoons and foxes—and from the goose with one foot. I never thought geese could be so mean.

Every day when I look out, I see the goose in the same place. Bending over to get at the grass. Balancing her weight the way a ballerina would. Now even Henry knows she's different, and doesn't chase her.

I want to feed her. Pet her. Be her friend. But
Mama says I mustn't. "A wild goose has to learn to
live with her weakness. Or she won't live at all."

"Try to be strong, little girl," Papa tells me,
"and let her be." But being strong is hard.

When Mama and Papa aren't looking, I sneak
my goose some cracked corn. I talk to her like Mama
talks to me when I'm sick. Soft and quiet. "I'm so
sorry, goose. Does it hurt? Don't be afraid."

Then I tell her a story like Papa tells me before
I go to bed. I blow her a kiss, and whisper, "Try to
be strong, little goose."

One day when I look out, I don't see the goose with one foot. I run outside—and there she is—over where the grass is greener—hobbling on her stumpy leg. Like my grandma with her cane.

"Atta girl," I whisper, the way my teacher does when I try something hard at school.

The next day I tell her that I'm learning to swim.
"But it's not as hard as learning to walk is for you,"
I say. And she listens.

Another day, *she* tries to swim. Slowly at first.
Then faster. Paddling across the **deserted** pond.
Deserted except for me and Henry. Cheering.

"If only she would fly," I tell Mama. "Then the other geese wouldn't think she's weak. And she wouldn't always be by herself."

"It's not so easy," Mama says.

"She'd have to push off pretty hard with one foot," Papa tells me.

"Come on, goose," I whisper. "It will be getting cold soon. How will you keep safe when the pond **freezes** over?"

But she doesn't even try to fly. All summer long,
my goose is happy to hobble and nibble and drink
and swim.

One day I notice that the other geese have started
swimming with her. Hooray! In the water, they look
just the same. But I know they aren't.

By September, it's almost time for the geese to fly south. And for me to go back to school. I wonder what will happen to the goose with one foot when the others fly away. I wish she would stay. And I wish she would go. Both at the same time.

"Who will be your friend when I'm at school?" I ask her.

One afternoon when I get home, the geese have gone. I scatter some corn, but no one comes to get it. Henry looks at me, and I look at Henry.

We don't know what to think. Except that our goose is gone, too.

All fall and winter, I think about my goose.
When I'm riding in the bus, I think I see her.
Picking apples, I think I hear her.

When I'm playing soccer,
I **imagine** how hard it would be
to run with one foot.

64

In November, I'm in a play at school.

In January, our pond is frozen solid. And in February, Mama starts her tomato plants indoors.

In March, Henry has begun to shed his winter coat. And Papa says I've grown two inches since summer.

I'm the first in my family to spot the red-breasted robin. The smell of onion grass is not far behind. Soon after, I feel the warm sun that turns the skating rink back into a pond.

Henry hears the honking first. He circles the pond, around and a half, mud splattering what's left of his winter coat. Henry knows the geese are coming, and then I know it, too.

FCAT Cause and Effect
How do the girl and Henry know that the geese are coming?

They land together. A couple of geese. Honking and flapping. Drinking and bathing. Combing each other's feathers. One is larger than the other, his neck as thick as a fire hose when he stretches it out to protect her—the goose with one foot.

"It's really you, goose!" I shout. "It's really you!"

For the rest of the spring, two geese swim and two geese sun. Two geese peck and two geese nibble. Side by side, they're always together. Like Henry and me. Friends.

Then one morning in May, I find a big surprise.
There is the goose with one foot and—seven babies!
Seven babies with fourteen feet. Peeping and prancing
and flapping and following. Right behind their papa.

I smile at the parade, and especially at my goose.
"Look at you," I whisper. "Look at you."

Meet the
Author and Illustrator

One day a few years ago, author **Cari Best** saw a one-footed goose in her yard. She didn't know how the goose lost its foot. She wondered whether it was from a snapping turtle, or perhaps an accident on the ice. But the goose with one foot did give Cari the idea for *Goose's Story*.

Collage artist **Holly Meade** says that making sketches is the hardest part of her job. "They involve answering a lot of important questions," she says. Holly has to think about what to put in the picture from the story, and what to add to the picture that's not in the story. She says it is important that her pictures "stay true to the spirit of the story."

FCAT **Write About It**

Cari Best tells a story about a goose. What is your favorite animal? Write about how you might take care of it if you had the chance.

Other books written by Cari Best

 LOG ON Find out more about Cari Best and Holly Meade at **www.macmillanmh.com**

72

 Comprehension Check

Retell the Story

Use the Retelling Cards to retell the story.

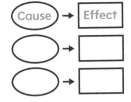

Retelling Cards

Think and Compare

1. How does the goose's injury change her life? Use information and details from the story to explain your answer. **Ask Questions: Cause and Effect**

2. Reread page 53. Why does the girl **balance** on one foot? **Analyze**

3. Why do you think the girl feeds corn to the goose? **Evaluate**

4. Why do you think the goose comes back to the pond the next spring? **Analyze**

5. How are the deserted geese in "Bill Helps Geese Survive" on pages 44–45 like the girl's goose? How are they different? **Reading/Writing Across Texts**

Science

Genre
Newspaper Articles give information and facts about current events.

Text Feature
Maps are drawings of places. They can help a reader understand where an article takes place.

Content Vocabulary

sanctuary

pollution

endangered

Baby Owl Rescue Is a "Hooting" Success!

by Bertie Benson

Sarasota, Florida — A baby owl fell out of its nest last week on Washington Boulevard. The bird got help from people at a bird **sanctuary**. A sanctuary is a place where animals are kept safe. Workers at the Pelican Man Bird Sanctuary treated the bird at their hospital. Then they returned the bird to its nest.

The baby owl fell 40 feet. Luckily, it was not hurt badly. Workers at the hospital fed the bird. They kept it warm and safe. The tiny owl looked like a fluffy white ball. Its eyes had not opened yet.

The workers asked a tree service to help them put the bird back in its nest. The tree service used a crane with a long neck. A man carefully put the baby owl back. The workers think the other baby might have accidentally pushed the baby bird out of its nest.

The team went back after two days to check on the baby owl. Its parents were feeding and taking care of it. The baby owl was safe.

The sanctuary was started by Dale Shields. Dale was called the "Pelican Man" because at first he only helped pelicans. Later he and his helpers started saving any animal in need. So far they have helped birds, deer, raccoons, bats, foxes, bobcats, turtles, and frogs.

Dale Shields

Wild animals get hurt in many ways. Water birds are injured when they get tangled in fishing lines. Animals are also hit by cars or boats. Water and land **pollution** hurts animals, too. Many of the animals the sanctuary helps are **endangered**. The workers want to help make sure the animals don't die out.

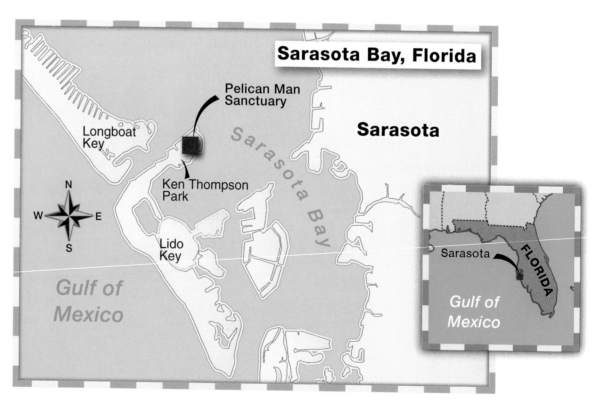

These maps show where the sanctuary is located in Florida. The area in red on both maps indicates the sanctuary.

People call the sanctuary when they see a hurt bird or other wildlife. Sanctuary workers go to pick up the animal. Then they take the animal to the hospital. Their work helps many animals survive.

Half of the animals the sanctuary helps are returned to the wild. Other animals, like Moe, need special care. Moe is a swan who was attacked by a dog. It lost one of its wings, so it can't fly. Today, Moe and other animals like him live at the sanctuary.

 FCAT Connect and Compare

1. Where in Florida is the sanctuary located? **Map**

2. Think about the newspaper article and *Goose's Story*. How are the stories alike? How are they different? **Reading/Writing Across Texts**

Science Activity

Research an endangered animal. Write about why the animal is endangered and what people are doing to help it.

LOG ON Find out more about animal rescue at **www.macmillanmh.com**

Important Details
Good writers include important details in their writing. This helps to make their message clear.

This detail is important.

Here is another good detail.

WRITE ABOUT AN EVENT

Sea Turtles Spotted at Cedar Beach
by Ken L.

People gathered at Cedar Beach yesterday to watch sea turtles come ashore. Every summer the sea turtles come to the beach to lay their eggs. Scientists told the crowd not to bother the turtles or their nests.

"People have helped the turtles by staying far away," Dr. Ralph Santos said. "It is not easy to see the nests, and people can step on them by accident."

Who people and Dr. Ralph Santos

What gathered on the beach

Where Cedar Beach
When yesterday

Why sea turtles spotted

Writing Prompt

A current event is a news story.

Think about a current event in your school or town.

Write about this current event.

FCAT Writer's Checklist

 Focus: My writing explains a current event.

 Organization: My writing includes a cause and effect.

 Support: I include important details that make my writing clear.

Conventions: I vary my sentences to make them more interesting to read. My spelling is correct.

Talk About It

How do people cause problems for Earth? What can people do to help?

LOG ON Find out more about ways to help Earth at **www.macmillanmh.com**

Helping Planet Earth

Prairie Dog

Vocabulary

conservation

remains

trouble

extinct

hardest

Prairie Problem

"We really do not have a lot of time left to save the prairie," says Ron Cole. A prairie is a large, flat area covered with grasses.

Prairies have very few trees. Prairies once stretched across the middle part of the United States. Today, most of that land is covered with farms and towns instead of grasses. Ron Cole belongs to a **conservation** group that teaches people to take better care of the prairie. Their goal is to protect the prairie land that **remains**. That will help the plants and animals that live there.

Ron Cole

A South Dakota prairie

BE CAREFUL!
WE'RE ALMOST GONE!

Experts warn us that many animals on our planet are in **trouble**. More than one thousand animal species are endangered! That means that they may disappear forever and become **extinct**.

It is natural for some plants and animals to become extinct. But now humans are causing more living things to become extinct than ever before. As people cut down forests, mow down prairies, or move into deserts, plants and wild animals get pushed out.

Protecting endangered species is one of the **hardest** jobs people face. The good news is that people are working to solve this problem before it gets worse.

California Condor, an endangered species

Endangered Animals

Amphibians: about 30 species

Insects: about 50 species

Fish: about 130 species

Birds: about 275 species

Mammals: about 350 species

This chart shows the number of animal species that are endangered.

LOG ON Find out more about endangered animals at **www.macmillanmh.com**

A Way to Help Planet Earth

Comprehension

Genre
A **Nonfiction Article** gives information about real people, things, or events.

Ask Questions
FCAT Main idea and Details
A description gives information about what something is like.

What can everyone do to help keep Earth clean?

Keeping Earth healthy is an important job. That's what environmental **conservation** is all about. People who do that job are working to keep the air, land, and water clean. They are also working to keep endangered plants and animals from becoming **extinct**.

One of the **hardest** jobs is solving the problem of trash. The **trouble** with trash is that it keeps piling up. We could run out of places to put it.

Plastic bottles are piled high at recycling centers.

84

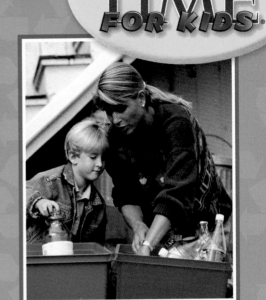

A lot of our trash comes from plastic. Soda, juice, water, shampoo—these all come in plastic bottles. Too much plastic is one of our worst trash problems. When a plastic bottle becomes trash, it **remains** trash for hundreds of years. That's because plastic doesn't change much as it gets old.

Is there a better way to deal with plastic? Yes! We can recycle it.

When we recycle, we take something that's been used and turn it into something new. An old plastic bottle can stay old and become trash. Or that old plastic bottle can be recycled and become something new.

People recycle plastic and glass at home and at school.

85

1 Plastic bottles are separated from other trash.

2 Sanitation trucks collect the recyclables.

3 Plastics are taken to a recycling center.

4 Bottles are crushed into small pieces.

Here's how it works. People save their plastic bottles. A special recycling truck picks the bottles up and takes them to the recycling center. Here, the bottles are crushed into small pieces. Then the small pieces of plastic are melted down. The melted plastic is sent to a factory.

At the factory, the old plastic is made into something new. It may become a new bottle or maybe a new rug. It may become a backpack or maybe even a slide at a playground!

5 A factory turns recycled plastic into something new and useful.

A teacher and students visit a recycling center.

Sometimes there's not much kids can do to help solve our planet's problems. But kids can do a lot about trash. Recycling is one way all people, young and old, can make a big difference!

FCAT
Think and Compare

1. Why is plastic trash a problem?

2. Describe what Earth would look like without recycling.

3. Besides recycling plastic, what does your community do to help keep Earth clean?

4. Prairies are smaller, some animals are endangered, and too much plastic is being thrown away. How have humans caused these problems?

Right There
The answer is right there on the page. Skim for clues to find the answer.

WATER TROUBLES

Cormelia Gogu lives in Romania. Last year her school did not have clean water to drink. The water pipes were old and rusty. Workers from several countries replaced the pipes so Cormelia's school now has clean water.

Cormelia doesn't take water for granted. But many people do. In the United States, we can just turn on a faucet to get clean water. It isn't that easy in other countries.

Most of Earth is covered with water. But only a small amount is safe to drink. Some places receive little rainfall, so there isn't enough water to grow crops. In other places, the water is so dirty that it is not safe to drink.

Groups such as the United Nations are working to solve these problems. People need to save water so that everyone has water to drink.

These boys in Guatemala are enjoying clean water from a tap for the first time.

Go on ▶

FCAT **Now answer Numbers 1 through 4. Base your answers on the article "Water Troubles."**

1 Why is some water not safe to drink?

- Ⓐ It comes from rain.
- Ⓑ It is too old.
- Ⓒ It is too dirty.
- Ⓓ It does not taste good.

Tip
Skim for clues.

2 Why should you save water?

- Ⓐ to keep water clean
- Ⓑ to help birds and animals
- Ⓒ so there is enough water to swim in
- Ⓓ so everyone has enough water to drink

3 Why don't some places have enough water?

- Ⓐ There are too many people.
- Ⓑ They receive little rainfall.
- Ⓒ There is too much rain.
- Ⓓ There are too many crops.

4 Describe what happened to the water at Cormelia Gogu's school. Use details and information from the article to support your answer.

READ
THINK
EXPLAIN

Write to a Prompt

Tom wrote several paragraphs explaining how he would take care of Earth's resources.

I told my main idea at the beginning of the essay. Then I used details to support it.

We All Need the Earth

Earth has many resources. We have land, water, and air. We need to take care of these parts of Earth. We need to keep them clean.

Farmers use land to grow crops. If we put poison in the ground, crops will not grow. If we put buildings on all the land, there will be no farms. We need to save land.

We all need water. We drink it and use it to stay clean. But people waste water. If we run out of water, we cannot live.

We have to take care of the air, too. We need clean air to breathe. If we stop driving cars so much, the air will be cleaner.

We all need to save Earth's resources.

Your Writing Prompt

Now it's your turn to write an essay telling people to take care of our environment.

FCAT There are many ways to care for the environment.

Think about what people can do.

Now write about what people can do to keep our land, water, and air clean.

Writing Hints for Prompts

- ☑ Think about your purpose for writing.

- ☑ Form an opinion about the topic.

- ☑ Use details to support your main idea.

- ☑ Be sure your ideas are logical and organized.

Wild Weather

Wild

Weather Hits Florida

by Lisa O'Neil

Hurricane Charley hit Florida in 2004. It was a **violent** storm that caused a lot of damage.

News reports told people in Florida to **beware** of the storm. People had to watch out for heavy rains and strong winds. Some people tried to make sure that their homes were safe. They covered their windows with wooden boards. The boards **prevent** windows from breaking.

Heavy rains dumped water everywhere and caused floods. Powerful winds **uprooted** trees.

The trees were blown over and the roots came out of the ground. Strong winds were even able to **destroy** houses. Some were completely flattened. Hurricane Charley also damaged crops. Luckily it did not hurt any of the cows in the **grasslands**. Farmers took the animals off the grassy fields in time.

Reread for **Comprehension**

Reread

FCAT Cause and Effect

Rereading an article can help you confirm **predictions,** or check guesses you made, about what will happen later in the article. Reread the article and use the chart to make and confirm predictions about the weather.

What I Predict	What Happens

Comprehension

Genre
Nonfiction gives information and facts about a topic.

Reread

Cause and Effect
As you read the selection, use the **Prediction** Chart.

What I Predict	What Happens

Read to Find Out
What is it like when there is a super storm?

SUPER STORMS

by Seymour Simon

The air around us is always
moving and changing.
We call these changes weather.

Storms are sudden, **violent** changes in the weather.

Every second, hundreds of thunderstorms are born around the world. Thunderstorms are heavy rain showers. They can drop millions of gallons of water in just one minute.

FCAT Cause and Effect
How might a thunderstorm cause damage?

During a thunderstorm lightning bolts can shoot between clouds and the ground. A bolt of lightning is 50,000 degrees. That's five times hotter than the surface of the sun. Lightning can destroy a tree or a small house. It can also start fires in forests and grasslands.

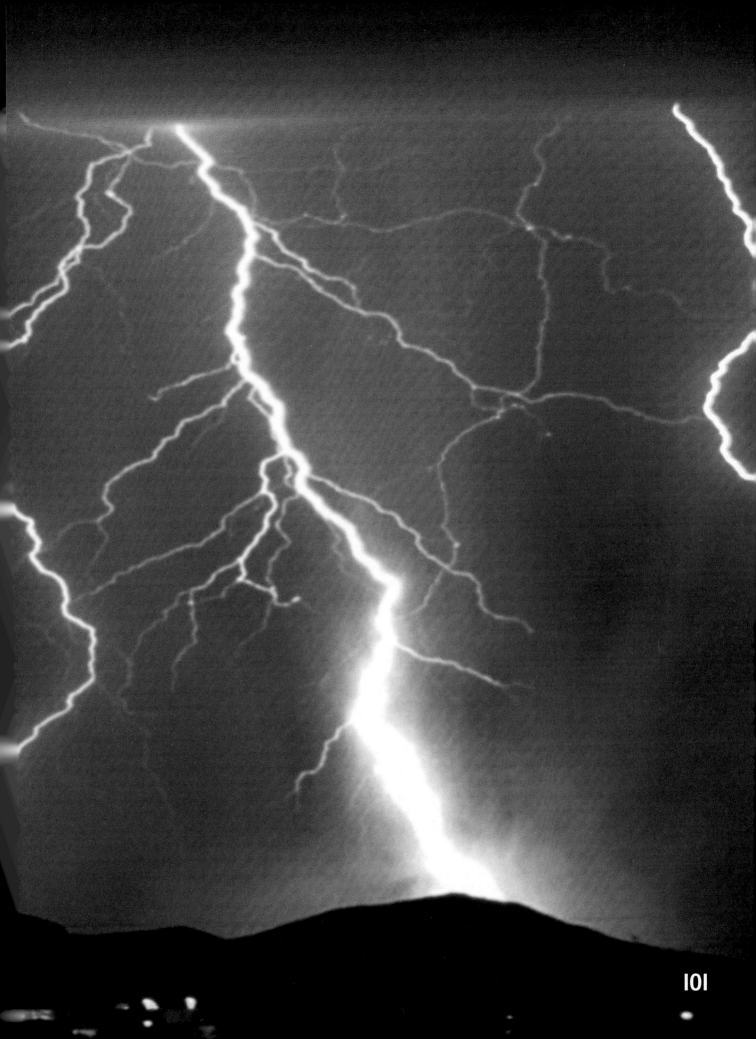

Thunder is the sound lightning
makes as it suddenly heats the air.
You can tell how far away lightning is.
Count the seconds between the flash of
light and the sound of thunder.
Five seconds equal one mile.

103

Hailstones are chunks of ice that are tossed up and down by the winds of some thunderstorms.

Nearly 5,000 hailstorms strike the United States every year. They can destroy crops and damage buildings and cars.

Hail can be the size of a marble or larger than a baseball.

In July 1995, a fast-moving
group of thunderstorms hit
New York State. Winds reached
speeds of 100 miles per hour.
Over 3,000 lightning bolts
struck in one minute.
And millions of trees were
uprooted or snapped in two.

Thunderstorms sometimes
give birth to tornadoes.
Inside a storm, a funnel-shaped
cloud reaches downward.
Winds inside a tornado can spin
faster than 300 miles per hour.
These winds can lift cars off the
ground and rip houses apart.

More than 1,000 tornadoes strike the United States each year. Most of them form during spring and summer. In April 1974, nearly 150 tornadoes struck 13 states east of the Mississippi River. More than 300 people were killed and 5,000 were injured. Nearly 10,000 homes were destroyed.

Television and radio stations often give early alerts. A tornado watch means that one may strike during the next few hours.

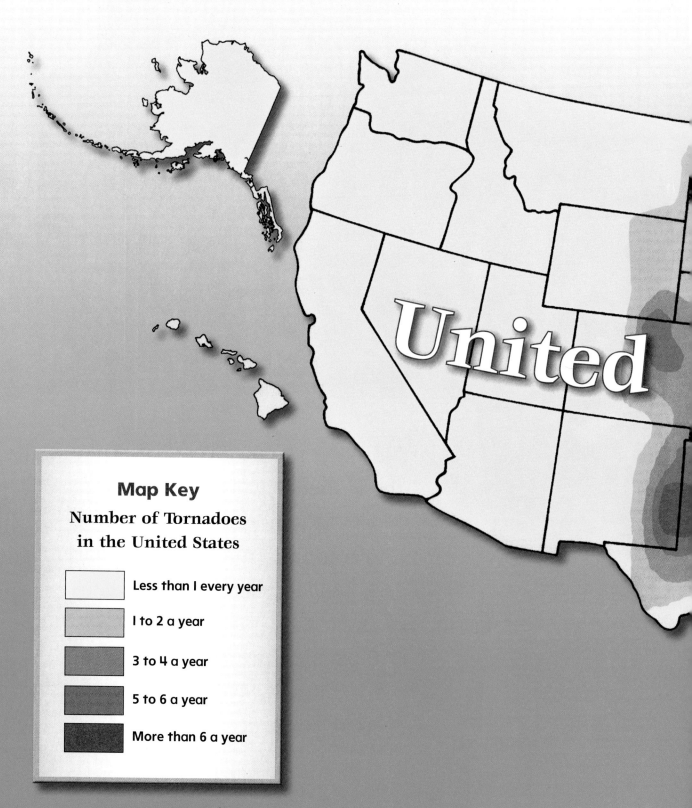

Map Key

Number of Tornadoes in the United States

Less than I every year

I to 2 a year

3 to 4 a year

5 to 6 a year

More than 6 a year

A warning means a tornado has been seen by people or on radar. During a tornado warning you should find shelter in a basement or closet.

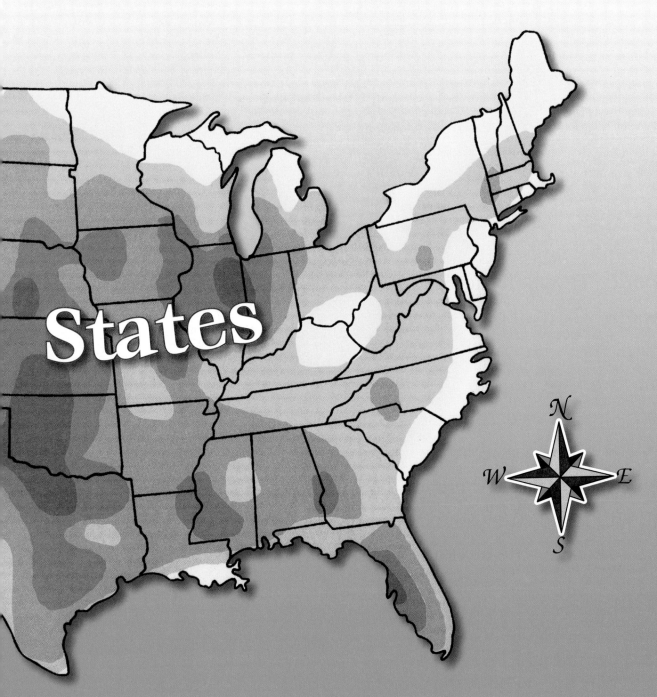

States

The map shows the number of tornadoes that hit the United States every year.

This photograph of a hurricane was taken in space looking at Earth.

Hurricanes are the deadliest storms in the world. They kill more people than all other storms combined. Hurricanes stretch for hundreds of miles. They have winds of between 74 and 200 miles per hour. The eye of a hurricane is the quiet center of the storm. Inside the eye, the wind stops blowing, the sun shines, and the sky is blue. But **beware**, the storm is not over yet.

 FCAT Cause and Effect
Why do you think the eye of a hurricane is dangerous?

Hurricanes are born over warm ocean waters from early summer to mid-fall. When they finally reach land, their pounding waves wash away beaches, boats, and houses.

Their howling winds bend and uproot trees and telephone poles. Their heavy rains cause floods.

In August 1992, Hurricane
Andrew smashed into Florida and
Louisiana. Over 200,000 people
were left homeless.

In the Pacific Ocean, hurricanes
are called typhoons. In April
1991, a typhoon hit the country of
Bangladesh. Over a million homes
were damaged or destroyed.
More than 130,000 people died.

Blizzards are huge snowstorms.
They have winds of at least
35 miles per hour. Usually
at least two inches of snow
falls per hour. Temperatures
are at 20 degrees or lower.
Falling and blowing snow make
it hard to see in a blizzard.

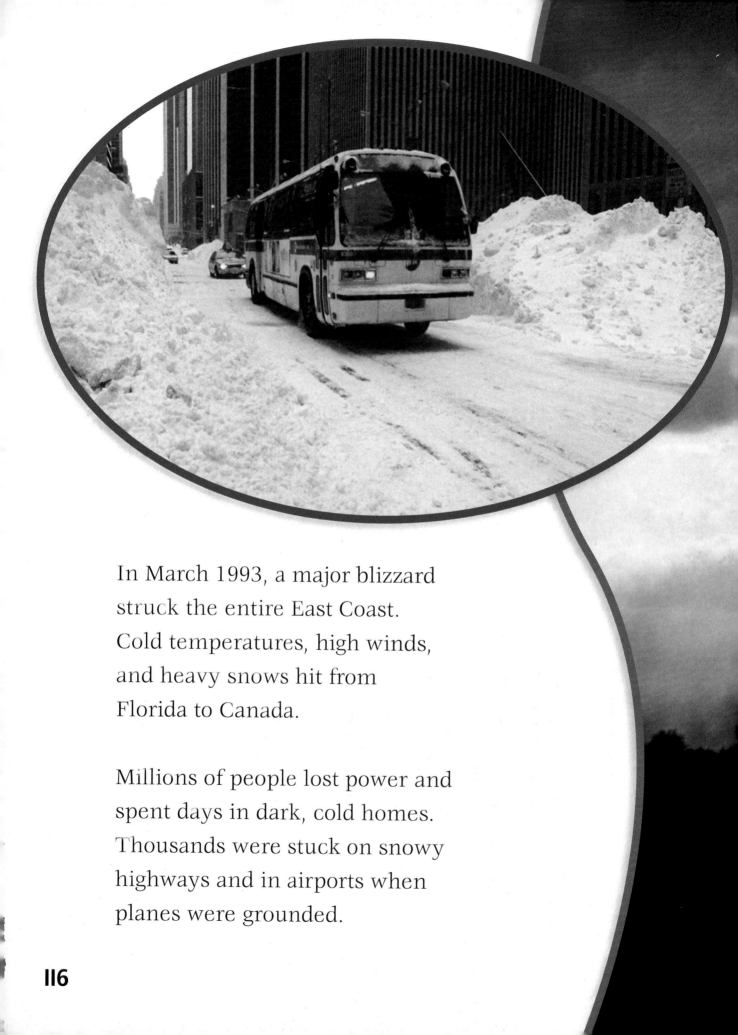

In March 1993, a major blizzard struck the entire East Coast. Cold temperatures, high winds, and heavy snows hit from Florida to Canada.

Millions of people lost power and spent days in dark, cold homes. Thousands were stuck on snowy highways and in airports when planes were grounded.

No one can prevent storms. But weather reports can predict and warn us when a storm may hit. The more prepared we are, the safer we will be when the next one strikes.

117

Science Facts about Seymour Simon

Seymour Simon has been writing about science for children for more than 40 years. He has written more than 200 books and is working on many more. He says that he'll never stop writing.

Seymour gets his ideas from many places. He says he was always interested in science. For example, Seymour wrote a book called *Pets in a Jar* because he collected little animals in jars as a boy. Other ideas come from his years as a science teacher. Now his grandchildren give him ideas. One grandson asked for a book about trains. *Seymour Simon's Book of Trains* was published soon after.

Other books written by Seymour Simon

 Find out more about Seymour Simon at www.macmillanmh.com

Gorillas

DESTINATION: MARS

FCAT Author's Purpose

Seymour Simon writes about storms. Think about a big storm that you watched. Write a paragraph that describes this storm.

FCAT Comprehension Check

Retell the Story

Use the Retelling Cards to retell the selection.

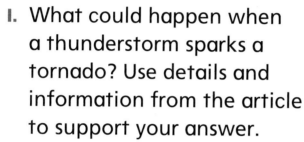

Retelling Cards

Think and Compare

READ THINK EXPLAIN

1. What could happen when a thunderstorm sparks a tornado? Use details and information from the article to support your answer. **Reread: Cause and Effect**

What I Predict	What Happens

2. Reread pages 110–111. What can you do to **prevent** problems from storms? **Apply**

3. What might happen if a blizzard was to hit your town? **Synthesize**

4. Why is it important for people to study different weather conditions? **Evaluate**

5. What new information about hurricanes did you find in "Wild Weather Hits Florida" on pages 94–95 that was not in *Super Storms*? **Reading/Writing Across Texts**

Poetry

Genre

Poems can describe a place by using strong words that help form a picture in your mind.

Literary Elements

Repetition is when one word or phrase appears two or more times in a poem.

Word Choice is important in a poem. The words a poet uses give the poem a certain feeling or mood.

It Fell in the City

by Eve Merriam

It fell in the city,
It fell through the night,
And the black rooftops
All turned white.

Red fire hydrants
All turned white.
Blue police cars
All turned white.

Green garbage cans
All turned white.
Gray sidewalks
All turned white.

Yellow NO PARKING signs
All turned white.
When it fell in the city
All through the night.

 FCAT Connect and Compare

1. What phrases are repeated in this poem? Why do you think the author uses so many color words? **Repetition and Word Choice**

2. Think about this poem and *Super Storms*. Which kind of storm is the storm in the poem most like? Explain why. **Reading/Writing Across Texts**

LOG ON   Find out more about weather at **www.macmillanmh.com**

Vary Sentences
Good writers vary the sentence lengths and types of sentences they write to make their writing more interesting.

Write About Weather

I begin my writing with a statement.

Here I write a question to vary my sentences.

Rain and Snow
by Pedro V.

Rain and snow are kinds of weather. Both give living things the water they need. Did you know that both rain and snow form because of the water cycle? When clouds have too much water, the water falls to Earth as rain or snow. The big difference between snow and rain is temperature. It must be below freezing for snow to fall. If it is above freezing, it rains.

Writing Prompt

Everyone has had experiences with weather.

Think about what you know about different kinds of weather.

Write a paragraph about two kinds of weather.

FCAT Writer's Checklist

✓ **Focus:** My writing clearly compares two kinds of weather.

☐ **Organization**: I vary sentence types and lengths to make my writing interesting.

✓ **Support**: I include details that support the main ideas of my writing.

✓ **Conventions**: The end punctuation of my sentences is correct. I use capital letters in the right places.

HABITATS AND HOMES

Talk About It

How are habitats different for animals and humans?

LOG ON Find out more about habitats and homes at **www.macmillanmh.com**

Vocabulary

beloved

promised

wiggled

gleamed

glanced

noble

FCAT **Word Parts**

Word endings added to the end of a verb can tell you when an event took place. The ending –ed shows that the action was in the past.

gleam + ed = gleamed

My Home in Alaska

Dear Katie,

I am so happy to meet my new pen pal! I live in an Eskimo village in Alaska. I live with my parents and my **beloved** grandfather. I love him more than almost anybody!

I want to tell you about going with Grandpa to the tundra near my home. Grandpa had **promised** to show me a wolf. Last Sunday he kept his word.

We got up early. I put on my heavy sweater and **wiggled** into my boots. They were a tight fit so I moved my feet quickly from side to side to get them on.

Grandpa and I traveled by dog sled. The snow **gleamed** in the sun. It shone so bright that we wore sunglasses. We stopped on a frozen lake. Grandpa **glanced** around, looking quickly in each direction. Then his eyes stopped. I looked at the same place. A wolf pack was near the lake. The **noble** wolves stood together. They looked impressive and as proud as kings. I will never forget those amazing animals.

Your new friend,

Jean

Reread for **Comprehension**

Reread

Plot

Rereading a story and using what you already know can help you figure out something, or **make an inference**, about a character. Reread the selection and use the chart to help you make inferences about Jean.

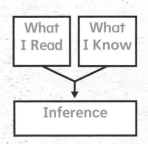

Comprehension

Genre
Fiction is a story with made-up characters and events.

FCAT Reread
Plot

As you read, use your Inference Chart.

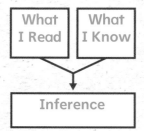

Read to Find Out
How do you know the boy and the wolf pup have a close friendship?

128

Nutik, the Wolf Pup

by Jean Craighead George
illustrated by Ted Rand

Award Winning Author

129

In an Eskimo village at the top of the world lived a lively little boy. He was not very old, but he could run as fast as a bird's shadow.

When he ran, his father, Kapugen, the great hunter, caught him and lifted him high over his head.

When he ran, his mother, Ellen, caught him and hugged him closely.

When he ran, his big sister, Julie, caught him and carried him home to tell him wolf stories.

She told him how a wolf pack had saved her life
when she was lost and starving on the vast tundra.
The wolf pack's **noble** black leader had shared his
family's food with her.

The wolf's name was Amaroq.

The little boy's name was Amaroq.

One day Julie came home with two pups. They were hungry and sickly. She put one in Amaroq's arms.

"Feed and tend this pup," she said. "His name is Nutik. I will feed and tend the other pup. I named her Uqaq. When they are fat and well, the wolves will come and get them."

Amaroq hugged his pup. He felt the little wolf heart beat softly. He kissed the warm head.

"Amaroq," Julie said when she saw this, "do not come to love this wolf pup. I have **promised** the wolves we will return the pups when they are fat and well."

Amaroq looked into Nutik's golden eyes. The wolf pup licked him and wagged his tail. Julie frowned.

"Don't fall in love, Amaroq," she warned again, "or your heart will break when the wolves come and take him away."

"No, it won't," he said.

FCAT Plot

Do you think Amaroq will begin to love the wolf pup? Why or why not?

134

Julie gave Amaroq a bottle of milk to feed to his pup. Amaroq wrapped Nutik in soft rabbit skins, and they snuggled down on the grizzly-bear rug.

Every day Amaroq fed Nutik many bottles of milk, bites of raw meat, and bones to chew.

When the moon had changed from a crescent to a circle and back again, Nutik was fat. His legs did not wobble. His fur **gleamed**. He bounced and woofed. When Amaroq ran, Nutik ran.

Summer came to the top of the world. The sun stayed up all day and all night for three beautiful months.

Because of this, Amaroq and Nutik lived by a different clock.

They fell asleep to the gabble of baby snow geese. They awoke to the raspy hiss of snowy owlets.

They ate when they were hungry. They slept when they were tired, and they played wolf games in shadow and sun. They were never apart.

"Don't fall in love with Nutik," Julie warned again when the midnight sun was riding low. "I hear the wolves calling. Soon they will come for their pups." She looked at him. "Be strong."

"I am strong," he answered. "I am Amaroq."

One morning Amaroq and Nutik were tumbling on the mossy tundra when the wolf pack called. They were close by.

"Come home. Come home," they howled.

Nutik heard them.

Uqaq and Julie heard them.

Amaroq heard them. He got to his feet and ran.

Nutik stopped listening to the wolves and ran after him.

Amaroq led Nutik as fast as a falling star. He led him down a frost heave. He led him around the village schoolhouse. He led him far from the wolves.

After a long time he led Nutik home. Julie was at the door.

"Uqaq has returned to her family," she said. "The wolves came and got her. Nutik is next."

"I am very tired," Amaroq said, and he rubbed his eyes.

Julie put him to bed in his bearskin sleeping bag. When Julie tiptoed away, Nutik **wiggled** into the sleeping bag too. He licked Amaroq's cheek.

The sun set in August. The days grew shorter until there was no day at all. Now it was always nighttime.

In the blue grayness of the winter night the wolves came to the edge of the village.

When everyone was sleeping, they called to Nutik.

Nutik crawled out of Amaroq's sleeping bag and gently awakened him. He took his hand in his mouth and led him across the room. He stopped before Amaroq's parka. Amaroq put it on. Nutik picked up a boot. Amaroq put on his boots.

Nutik whimpered at the door.

Amaroq opened it. They stepped into the cold.

The wolves were prancing and dancing like ice spirits on the hill.

Nutik took Amaroq's mittened hand and led him toward his wolf family. The frost crackled under their feet. The wolves whispered their welcome.

Suddenly Amaroq stopped. Nutik was taking him to his wolf home.

"No, Nutik," he said. "I cannot go with you. I cannot live with your family." Nutik tilted his head to one side and whimpered, "Come."

"You must go home alone," Amaroq said, and hugged his **beloved** wolf pup for a long time.

Then he turned and walked away. He did not run. Nutik did not chase him.

"I am very strong," Amaroq said to himself.

He got home before his tears froze.

Amaroq crawled into his bearskin sleeping bag and sobbed. His heart was broken after all.

At last he fell asleep.

Julie awoke him for breakfast.

"I don't want to eat," he told her. "Last night the wolves came and took Nutik away."

"You are a strong boy," she said. "You let him go back to his family. That is right."

FCAT Plot

Why do you think Amaroq let Nutik return to his wolf pack?

Amaroq did not eat lunch. When Kapugen took him out to fish, he did not fish. Tears kept welling up. He ran home to hide them in his bearskin sleeping bag.

It was surprisingly warm.

Up from the bottom and into Amaroq's arms wiggled the furry wolf pup.

"Nutik," Amaroq cried joyfully. He hugged his friend and **glanced** at Julie. Instead of scolding him, she stepped outside.

"Dear wolves," she called across the tundra. "Your beautiful pup, Nutik, will not be coming back to you. He has joined our family.

"Amaroq loves Nutik. Nutik loves Amaroq. They are brothers now. He cannot leave."

As if listening, the wind stopped blowing. In the stillness Julie called out clearly and softly:

"I shall take care of him as lovingly as you took care of me."

And the wolves sang back, "That is good."

Meet the
Author and Illustrator

Jean Craighead George has written more than 100 children's books.

One summer, Jean went to Alaska to learn more about wolves. There, she saw a little girl walking on the lonely tundra. She also saw a beautiful male wolf. They became the characters for Jean's book *Julie of the Wolves*, for older readers. *Nutik, the Wolf Pup* is a follow-up to that book.

To draw the illustrations for *Nutik, the Wolf Pup*, **Ted Rand** went to Alaska. He wanted to see the tundra for himself. Ted has illustrated more than 60 children's books.

Other books written by Jean Craighead George

 Find out more about Jean Craighead George and Ted Rand at **www.macmillanmh.com**

FCAT Author's Purpose

Jean Craighead George tells a story about a boy and a wolf pup in an Eskimo village. Think about living in a village like Amaroq's. Would you like it? Why or why not? Write about this.

148

FCAT Comprehension Check

Retell the Story

Use the Retelling Cards to retell the story.

Retelling Cards

Think and Compare

READ
THINK
EXPLAIN

1. Julie **promised** the wolves she would return the pups, so why does she let Nutik stay with Amaroq in the end? Use details and information from the story to explain. **Reread: Plot**

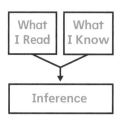

2. Reread pages 134–135. Why does Julie keep warning Amaroq not to love Nutik? **Analyze**

3. Why does Amaroq let Nutik return to his wolf pack? Would you have let the pup go? Why or why not? **Evaluate**

4. Why is it important for Nutik to return to his wolf family and not spend too long with Amaroq? **Analyze**

5. Do you think Jean in "My Home in Alaska," on pages 126–127, and Amaroq might be friends? What are some things that they have in common? **Reading/Writing Across Texts**

FLORIDA~ WILD in the USA

Many people live in Florida. Many animals live there, too. People sometimes cause changes in the **environment**. Some changes help the animals. Other changes are problems for them.

The Florida Panther

The Florida panther lives only in Florida. This panther is **endangered**. There are only about 60 Florida panthers left in the wild.

Panthers need a lot of space to hunt and raise their young. But more and more people are moving into the habitat of the panthers. This means there are fewer places for panthers to live in Florida.

Now people are trying to help the panthers. They have set aside places where the panthers' habitat is **protected**. They built fences and crossings on busy roads. These help to protect panthers.

This wildlife crossing helps to protect panthers from being hit by cars and trucks.

151

Manatees

Encyclopedia entries often have words in dark print called heads. These summarize what the following section will be about.

Florida manatees, or sea cows, live in warm water where sea grass grows, but they breathe air. These "gentle giants," which are related to elephants, have wrinkled gray-brown skin. They use their lips the way elephants use their trunks.

But manatees have lost much of their habitat. They are endangered. This is because people have moved to where the manatees live. The animals get tangled in fishing nets. Sometimes boats hit the manatees.

Now Florida has laws to protect these animals. Some people rescue hurt manatees. Some people teach others how to protect these animals.

People can help the Florida manatees.

Alligators

Florida is home to the American alligator, a large reptile related to the crocodile.

Alligators live in marshes, swamps, and other wetlands. But the way people use water can change these wetlands. This causes problems for alligators. To help, people in Florida are learning to share their environment with alligators.

FCAT Connect and Compare

1. In which section would you find information about where alligators live? What did you learn about in the section with the head "Manatees"? **Heads**

2. Think about the encyclopedia entry and *Nutik, the Wolf Pup*. Use this information to write a story about a child helping a manatee. **Reading/Writing Across Texts**

Science Activity

Research an animal that lives in Florida. Write facts about what the animal looks like, its habitat, and what it eats.

Find out more about Florida's Animals at **www.macmillanmh.com**

Write a Book Report

FCAT Writer's Craft

A Strong Conclusion
A good writer includes a **strong concluding sentence** at the end of a piece of writing.

My concluding sentence wraps up my report.

I give the title one final time.

A Report on Animals of the Sea and Shore

by Jan O.

I really liked <u>Animals of the Sea and Shore</u> by Ann O. Squire. The book describes many animals that live in or near the ocean. Some animals, like whales, live in the water. Other animals live on shore, like snails.

I also learned some unusual facts. Did you know that sea otters sleep floating on their backs? If you like learning about the creatures that live by the water, you'll like <u>Animals of the Sea and Shore</u>.

Writing Prompt

A book report gives information
about a book.

Think about a book that you have read.

Write a book report.

FCAT Writer's Checklist

✓ **Focus:** My book report clearly gives information about a book that I have read.

☑ **Organization:** I include a strong concluding sentence to completes my book report.

✓ **Support:** I include details that give the reader specific information about my book.

✓ **Conventions:** My spelling is correct. My sentences are complete.

Whale Watch →

Watching Whales

Becca's my best friend. That's why I said that I would go with her on a ship. To whale watch.

"How exciting can it be to watch big fish swim?" I asked Becca as we headed to the ship.

"It's thrilling!" Becca said. "But whales aren't fish. They're mammals. They're the biggest mammals on Earth. They are twenty times larger than elephants!"

"But they're not as interesting as elephants," I said. "Did you ever watch elephants take a shower by spraying water from their trunks?"

"Yes," Becca replied as we got on the ship. "But whales spout water through their blowholes. Some spouts are 30 feet high!"

"Whales can even leap out of water," Becca told me as the ship started to move.

"Leap out of the water?" I asked as we found a place to stand by the railing. "Do you mean they leap through the air like monkeys?"

"Well, not like monkeys," Becca said. "But whales sometimes jump into the air. Or they'll push their tails into the air. Did you know that every whale's tail is different—just like every zebra's stripes are different?"

"Look at that," someone shouted as the ship glided farther out into the sea. "A whale tail! See it over there?"

"Wow!" Becca yelled.

"WOW!" I yelled. "Ocean animals are exciting!"

157

The Story of the Umbrella

When do you use an umbrella? On rainy days, of course! Well, not if you lived a very long time ago. People used umbrellas only on sunny days.

The word *umbrella* means shade. An umbrella would shade you from the sun. Maybe that is why an umbrella is in the shape of a tree. A tree shades you from the sun.

There is another reason why umbrellas were just for sunny days. The first umbrellas were made of paper. You could never use one in the rain.

At first, only kings carried umbrellas. An umbrella made you look important. Thousands of years later, women started

People in the rain (in England) carrying umbrellas

England

carrying them. They used their paper umbrellas as shades from the sun. A hat on a stick was even used as an umbrella.

In England, oil was rubbed on paper umbrellas. The oil made the umbrellas waterproof so that they could be used in sun or rain.

Umbrellas are now used around the world. They are used by both men and women. Umbrellas keep people dry on rainy days. But they can still shade you on a sunny day—if you want them to!

LIFE IN THE DESERT

Talk About It

What is life like in the desert?

LOG ON Find out more about life in the desert at **www.macmillanmh.com**

THE COATIS OF THE SONORA DESERT

by Nya Taylor

Coatis (ko-WAH-tees) are animals that live in the desert. They look like raccoons and are about as big as cats. They have long tails that help them balance as they climb.

Coatis like to eat plants and insects. They use their claws to dig for small animals that may be living underground in a **burrow**. Some coatis eat while hanging from trees.

Coatis live together. They do not wander **beyond** their group. Staying close helps them hear **warning** calls if danger is near. Coatis spend hours taking **lengthy** rests in the shade. During the hot days, they need to stay cool. At night, they climb into trees to sleep.

You can see coatis at the Sonora Desert Museum in Arizona. The park has workers to help you. You may ask to use a **ranger's** binoculars to see far away. The binoculars will help you spot coatis in the trees in the **distant** mountains.

Reread for **Comprehension**

Summarize

Author's Purpose

One way to summarize an article is to explain the **author's purpose**. Ask yourself about the reasons why the author wrote this information. Reread the selection and use the chart to summarize the author's purpose.

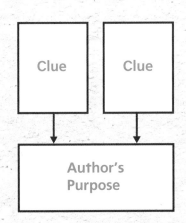

Clue	Clue

Author's Purpose

Comprehension

Genre

An **Informational Story** gives facts about a topic.

Summarize

Author's Purpose

As you read, use your **Author's Purpose** Chart.

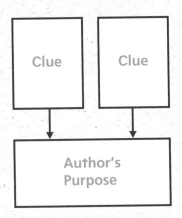

Clue	Clue

↓ ↓

Author's Purpose

Read to Find Out

What do you learn about the toad?

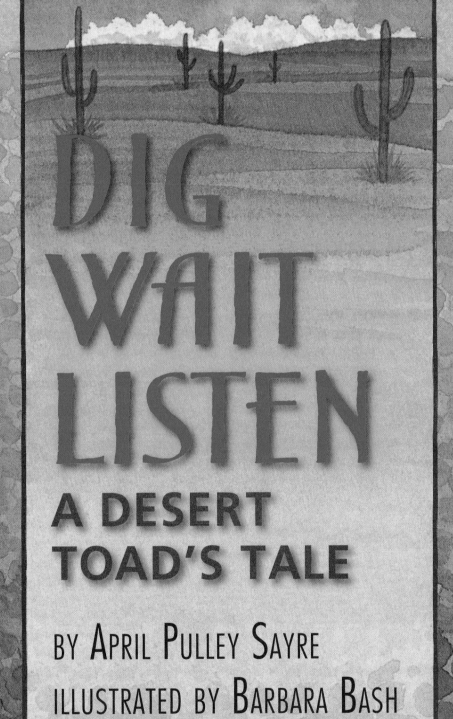

DIG WAIT LISTEN

A DESERT TOAD'S TALE

BY APRIL PULLEY SAYRE

ILLUSTRATED BY BARBARA BASH

Deep in the desert,
under the sand, the spadefoot
toad waits. She waits...for the
sound of rain.

Skitter, skitter, scratch.
She hears soft sounds.
Is this the rain at last?

No. It's the scorpion overhead,
crawling slowly past.
Skitter, scratch!

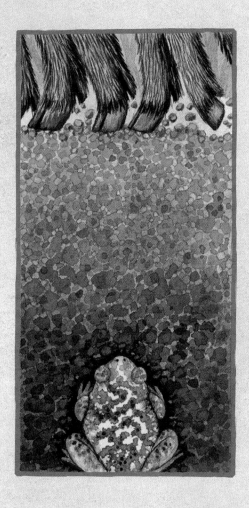

**Thunk, thunk, thunk.
Clink, clunk,
clink, clunk.**
Sounds shake the soil.

But it's only a herd of peccaries.
Their hooves hammer the ground.

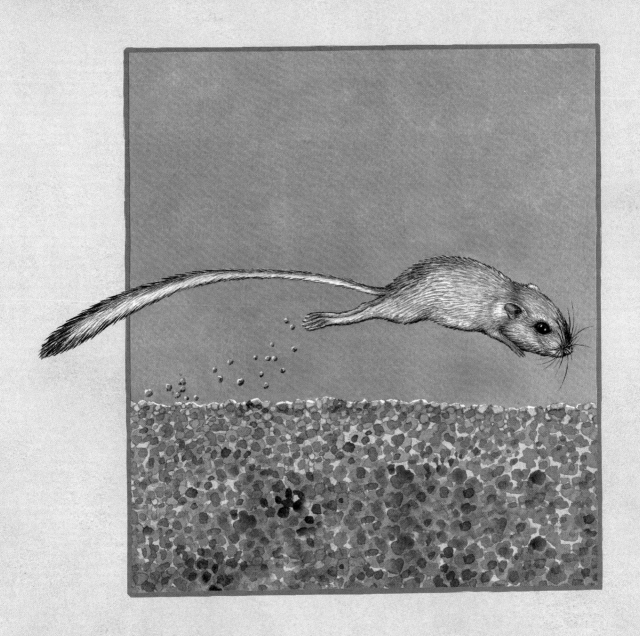

Pop, pop, pop.
What's that sound now?
Is this the rain at last?

No, it's a rat,
hopping in **lengthy** leaps
like a tiny kangaroo.

Will the rain *ever* come?
The desert's so hot, so dry!
And the toad's been waiting
so many months in her
basement **burrow** home.

FCAT **Author's Purpose**
Why do you think the author gives so much
information about the other desert animals?

Tap, tap, tap!
Could this be it?
Is this the rain at last?
No, it's a gila woodpecker
tapping on a tall green cactus.

171

The toad feels the ground begin to shake.
Then a **crunch, crunch, crunch**
that's loud.
Is this the rain?

No. It's a park ranger's boots
walking on the path.

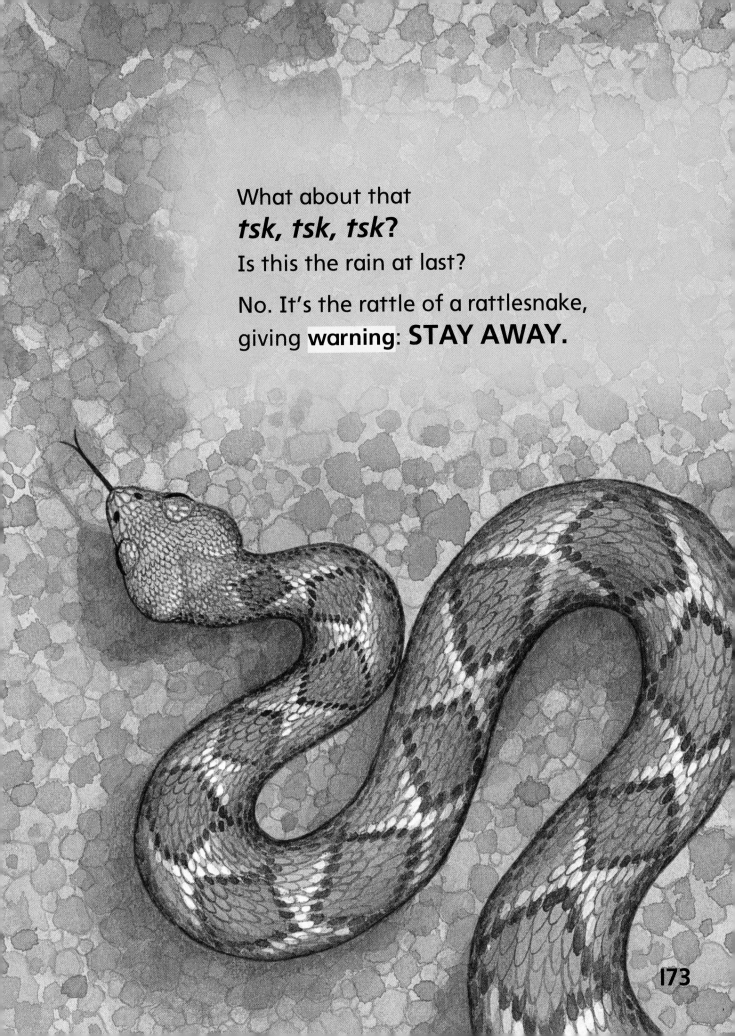

What about that
tsk, tsk, tsk?
Is this the rain at last?

No. It's the rattle of a rattlesnake,
giving warning: STAY AWAY.

Surely that rumbling…
that rumble, rumbling….
Surely that's the rain…?
Not yet.
It's the thunder of a **distant** storm.
But perhaps the rain is near.

174

Plip, plop, **plip,** plop.
Plip, plop, **plop!**
Is this the rain at last?
Plop **thunk.** Plop **thunk.**
Plop **thunk** *gussssshhhhhhh!*
It is rain!

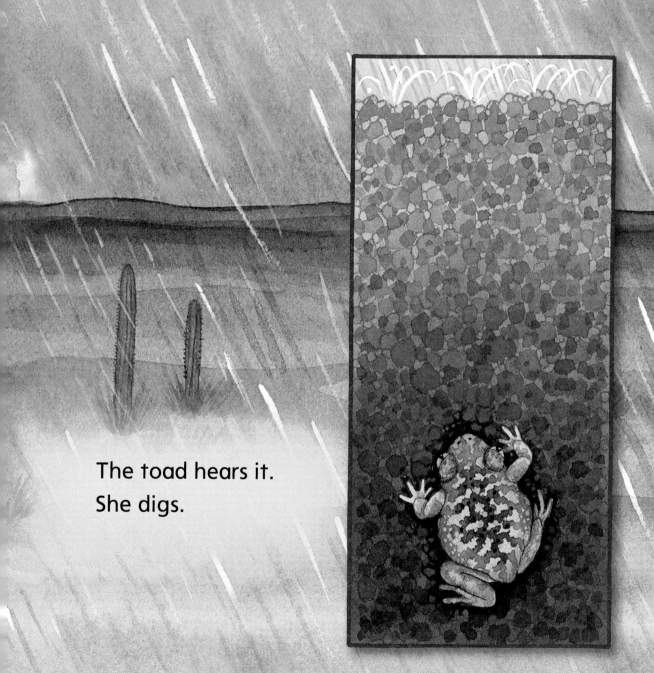

The toad hears it.
She digs.

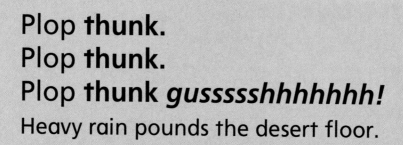

Plop **thunk.**
Plop **thunk.**
Plop **thunk** *gusssssshhhhhhh!*
Heavy rain pounds the desert floor.

Push, push, and the toad pops right out,
into the open air.

Bleat, bleat, bleat!
The toad hears loud bleats.
Is that the rain sound too?

No. It's male spadefoot toads,
calling: Here, come here!

Plop **thunk**. Plop **thunk**.
Plop **thunk**
gusssssshhhhhhh!
The toad hops in a puddle.
She lays her eggs,
like beads of glass.

Plop **thunk**, plop **thunk**, plop **thunk**
gussssshhhhhhh!

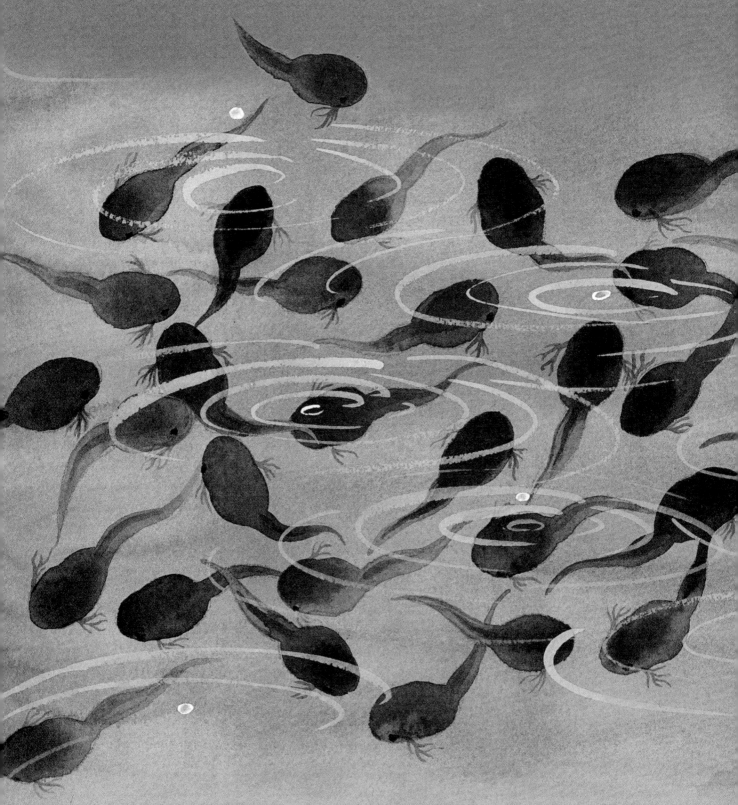

Two days later, the eggs hatch. Wriggling and wiggling in their puddle home, the tadpoles are here at last!

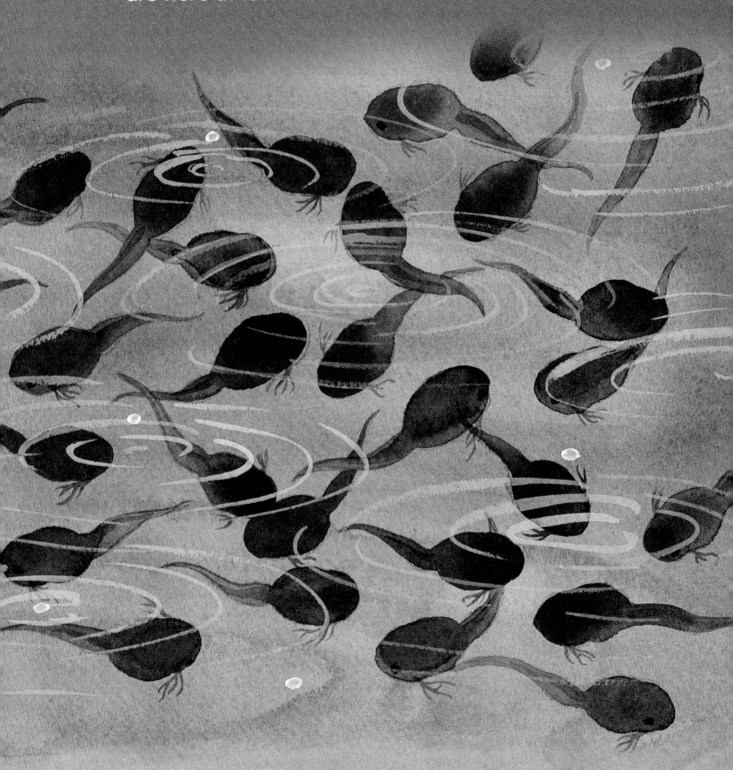

They eat.
They grow.
Legs start to show.
But their puddle is drying up!
Will any make it?

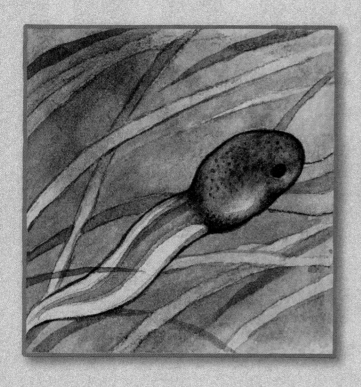

Yes!
With new legs formed,
young toads crawl
from their puddle home.
They rest, then

into the desert **beyond**.

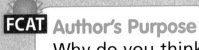

FCAT **Author's Purpose**
Why do you think the author
wrote this book? Explain.

Thump, thump, thump.

Hundreds of tiny toads jump.
The rain has made the desert green.

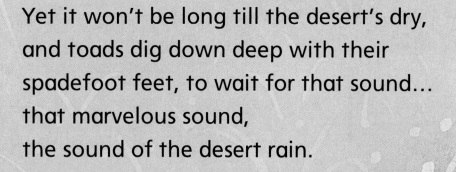

Yet it won't be long till the desert's dry,
and toads dig down deep with their
spadefoot feet, to wait for that sound…
that marvelous sound,
the sound of the desert rain.

Plop **thunk,** plop **thunk,**

plop **thunk** *gusssssshhhhhhh!*

Plop **thunk,** plop **thunk,**

plop **thunk** *gussssshhhhhhhh!*

Plop **thunk,** plop **thunk,**

plop **thunk** *gussssshhhhhhhh!*

ENJOY THE OUTDOORS WITH APRIL AND BARBARA

"I love writing—most of the time," says author **April Pulley Sayre**. "Sometimes my first try is horrible. But I rewrite until I like every paragraph. I try to communicate the excitement I feel about nature."

A love of nature also drives artist **Barbara Bash**. When she does research, she uses books and photos to get to know the topic. Next, Barbara visits the places in the stories. "Then," she says, "something alive and personal can be expressed through my books."

Other books written and illustrated by Barbara Bash

 LOG ON Find out more about April Pulley Sayre and Barbara Bash at **www.macmillanmh.com**

FCAT Author's Purpose

April Pulley Sayre teaches readers about desert toads. Think about an animal you know. Write about its life cycle, or all the parts of the animal's life.

FCAT Comprehension Check

Retell the Story

Use the Retelling Cards to retell the selection.

Retelling Cards

Think and Compare

1. What is the main message of this selection? Use details and information from the article to support your answer. **Summarize: Author's Purpose**

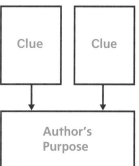

| Clue | Clue |

Author's Purpose

2. Reread pages 167–169. Why did the spadefoot toad think the noise she heard was rain? What was the noise? **Analyze**

3. Why might it be difficult for some animals to live in the desert? **Analyze**

4. How is a spadefoot toad's **burrow** like other animal homes? **Analyze**

5. How are the coatis in "The Coatis of the Sonoran Desert," on pages 162–163, and the spadefoot toad in *Dig, Wait, Listen* different? How are they alike? **Reading/ Writing Across Texts**

The Sonoran Desert

The Sonoran Desert is a dry area in the American Southwest. It covers about 100,000 square miles in parts of California, Arizona, and Mexico. Some parts of the Sonoran Desert may not have rain for one or two years. Other parts have sudden summer rainstorms.

Summer in the Sonoran Desert is very, very hot. The **temperature** is often more than 100 degrees during the day. Even in the winter, the temperature is usually above freezing.

Desert plants and animals have **adapted** to life in the desert. They have special ways to survive with very little water and in very hot weather.

Plants

The Sonoran Desert has many different kinds of cactus plants. Cactus plants can live a long time without rain.

Cactus plants store water in their thick stems. They also have thick, waxy leaves that help keep in water. Cactus roots grow close to the top of the ground. When it does rain, the roots can soak up the water very quickly.

Sonoran Desert Animals

Name	Type of Animal	What It Eats
black-chinned hummingbird	bird	flowers, nectar, nuts
coyote	mammal	small animals, insects, plants
ground snake	reptile	insects
horned toad	reptile	plants, insects
roadrunner	bird	insects, lizards, snakes
Sonoran Desert toad	amphibian	insects, mice

The animal name is in the first column.

Information about the animal is in the row.

Animals

Like desert plants, desert animals can live without much rain. Most desert animals do not have to drink water. They get the water they need from their food.

Many desert animals are **nocturnal**. This means they only come out to find food at night, when it is cool. During the hot days, these animals hide in the shade or underground. Staying cool helps animals keep water in their bodies.

FCAT Connect and Compare

1. Which desert animals eat insects? Which desert animals only eat plants? **Chart**

2. Think about this encyclopedia article and *Dig, Wait, Listen*. How is the spadefoot toad like the other animals of the Sonoran Desert? **Reading/Writing Across Texts**

 Science Activity

Use an encyclopedia to research desert plants. Make a chart that gives two facts for each plant.

LOG ON Find more desert facts at **www.macmillanmh.com**

Dialogue
Good writers use lively words in dialogue to make their characters sound interesting.

Quotation marks show dialogue.

This dialogue is interesting.

Write a Dialogue

Fox Tells a Joke
by Daniela M.

Fox liked to tell jokes. Tortoise liked Fox, so he put up with Fox's silly jokes.

"Tortoise," said Fox, "why can't it rain for two days without stopping?"

"I don't know," said Tortoise. "Is it because this is the desert?"

"No!" Fox laughed. "It's because there is always a night in between!" She laughed again. "Get it? A night is in between the two days!"

"Ha-ha. Very funny," said Tortoise. Then he pulled his head inside his shell.

Writing Prompt

Characters in a story can speak in their own words, or in dialogue.

Think about two characters from your writing.

Write a dialogue between these characters.

FCAT Writer's Checklist

☑ **Focus:** My writing clearly presents character dialogue.

✓ **Organization:** Each character's words are in a separate paragraph.

✓ **Support:** The details of each character's spoken words tell about him or her.

✓ **Conventions:** I use quotation marks correctly. I use capital letters in the proper places.

WHY SUN AND MOON LIVE IN THE SKY

Characters

Narrator   Moon

Sun   Water

Scene One: Sun and Moon's house

Narrator: Long ago Sun and Moon lived on Earth.

Moon: Sun, I see a **signal** in the sky. It is a sign.

Sun: Yes, clouds do not take those shapes **randomly**. The clouds don't look that way by accident. Water controls the clouds. I think he's asking me to visit.

Narrator: Sun and Water were friends. But Water never visited Sun and Moon's house.

Scene Two: The next day at Water's house

Sun: Water, please come visit our house.

Water: Your house is too small. I don't fit inside.

196

Sun: Moon and I will build a big new house so you can visit.

Scene Three: Sun and Moon's house

Narrator: Later, Sun told Moon his plan. Moon thought it was a good idea so she **agreed** to help. They decided to build the house with trees.

Moon: I **gathered** the wood and put it all together.

Sun: Please help me carry it. The ends keep **jabbing** and poking me.

Scene Four: Later at Sun and Moon's new house

Narrator: At last, Sun and Moon finished the house. It was time for Water to visit.

Water: Hello, friends. May I come in?

Narrator: Water entered the house and filled every corner. The house was still too small. There was no room left for Sun and Moon. So, they flew to the sky, where they still are today.

Reread for **Comprehension**

Visualize
FCAT Problem and Solution

Visualizing, or forming pictures in your mind, can help you understand the **problem and solution** in a story. Reread the play and use the chart to better understand the problem the characters faced and how they solved it.

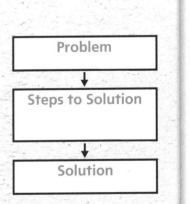

Problem
↓
Steps to Solution
↓
Solution

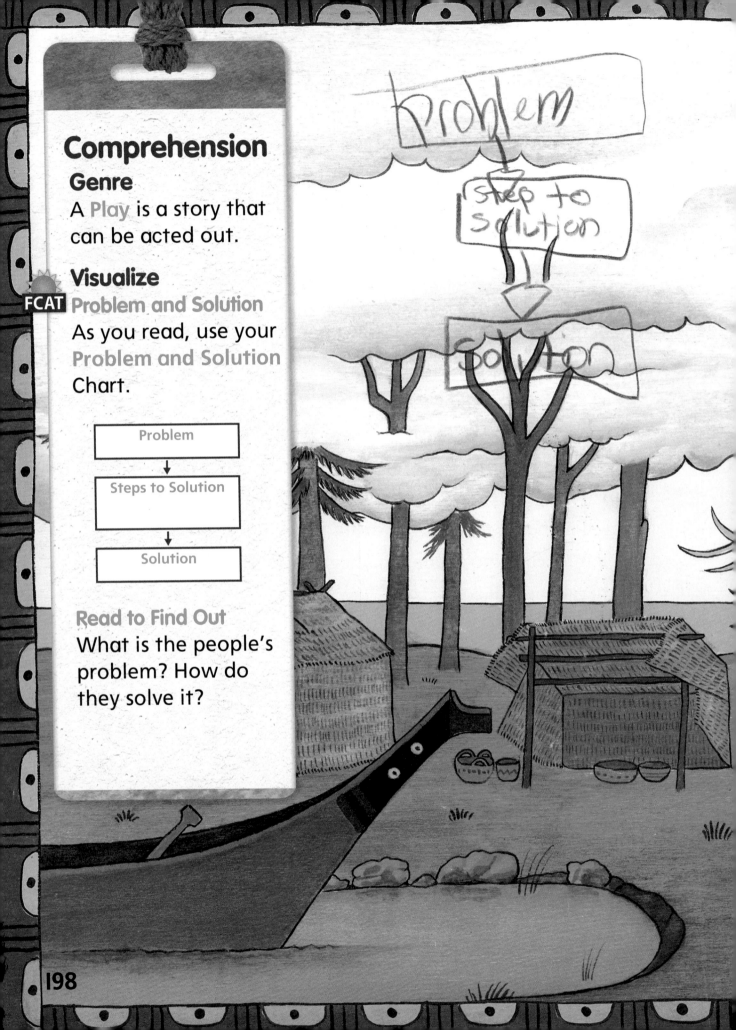

Comprehension

Genre
A **Play** is a story that can be acted out.

Visualize

Problem and Solution
As you read, use your **Problem and Solution** Chart.

Problem
↓
Steps to Solution
↓
Solution

Read to Find Out
What is the people's problem? How do they solve it?

Pushing Up the Sky

BY JOSEPH BRUCHAC

ILLUSTRATED BY STEFANO VITALE

Award Winning Author

SNOHOMISH

The Snohomish people lived in the area of the Northwest that is now known as the state of Washington. They fished in the ocean and **gathered** food from the shore. Their homes and many of the things they used every day, such as bowls and canoe paddles, were carved from the trees.

Like many of the other peoples of the area, they also carved totem poles, which recorded the history and stories of their nation. *Pushing Up the Sky* is a Snohomish story carved into a totem pole in Everett, Washington.

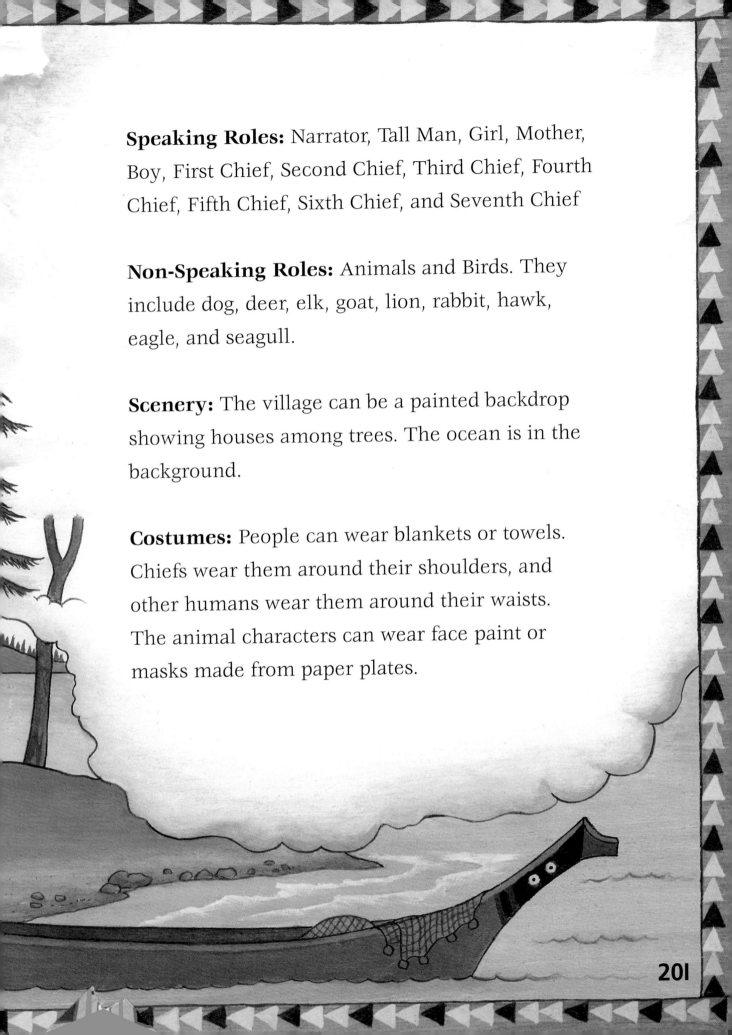

Speaking Roles: Narrator, Tall Man, Girl, Mother, Boy, First Chief, Second Chief, Third Chief, Fourth Chief, Fifth Chief, Sixth Chief, and Seventh Chief

Non-Speaking Roles: Animals and Birds. They include dog, deer, elk, goat, lion, rabbit, hawk, eagle, and seagull.

Scenery: The village can be a painted backdrop showing houses among trees. The ocean is in the background.

Costumes: People can wear blankets or towels. Chiefs wear them around their shoulders, and other humans wear them around their waists. The animal characters can wear face paint or masks made from paper plates.

SCENE 1: A Village Among Many Tall Trees
Tall Man, Girl, Mother, and Boy stand onstage.

Narrator: Long ago the sky was very close to the earth. The sky was so close that some people could jump right into it. Those people who were not good jumpers could climb up the tall fir trees and step into the sky. But people were not happy that the sky was so close to the earth. Tall people kept bumping their heads on the sky. And there were other problems.

Tall Man: Oh, that hurt! I just hit my head on the sky again.

Girl: I just threw my ball, and it landed in the sky. I can't get it back.

Mother: Where is my son? Has he climbed a tree and gone up into the sky again?

Boy: Every time I shoot my bow, my arrows get stuck in the sky!

All: THE SKY IS TOO CLOSE!

SCENE 2: The Same Village

The seven chiefs stand together onstage.

Narrator: So people decided something had to be done. A great meeting was held for all the different nations. The seven wisest chiefs got together to talk about the problem.

First Chief: My people all think the sky is too close.

Second Chief: A very good job was done of making the world.

Third Chief: That is true, but the sky should have been put up higher. My tall son keeps hitting his head on the sky.

Fourth Chief: My daughter keeps losing her ball in the sky.

Fifth Chief: People keep going up into the sky when they should be staying on the earth to help each other.

Sixth Chief: When mothers look for their children, they cannot find them because they are up playing in the sky.

Seventh Chief: We are **agreed**, then. The sky is too close.

All: WE ARE AGREED.

FCAT Problem and Solution
Why do the chiefs think the sky is too close to the ground?

Second Chief: What can we do?

Seventh Chief: I have an idea. Let's push up the sky.

Third Chief: The sky is heavy.

Seventh Chief: If we all push together, we can do it.

Sixth Chief: We will ask the birds and animals to help. They also do not like it that the sky is so close.

Second Chief: The elk are always getting their antlers caught in the sky.

Fourth Chief: The birds are always hitting their wings on it.

First Chief: We will cut tall trees to make poles. We can use those poles to push up the sky.

Fifth Chief: That is a good idea. Are we all agreed?

All: WE ARE ALL AGREED.

SCENE 3: The Same Village

*All the people, except Seventh Chief, are gathered together. They hold long poles. The Birds and Animals are with them. They all begin pushing **randomly**. They are **jabbing** their poles into the air. (The sky can be imagined as just above them.)*

Girl: It isn't working!

Boy: The sky is still too close.

Fifth Chief: Where is Seventh Chief? This was his idea!

Seventh Chief (entering): Here I am. I had to find this long pole.

FCAT **Problem and Solution**
Why doesn't the first plan to solve the problem work?

First Chief: Your plan is not good! See, we are pushing and the sky is not moving.

Seventh Chief: Ah, but I said we must push together.

Fifth Chief: We need a **signal** so that all can push together. Our people speak different languages.

Seventh Chief: Let us use YAH-HOO as the signal. Ready?

All: YES!

209

Seventh Chief: YAH-HOO.

At the signal everyone pushes together.

All: YAH-HOO!

Seventh Chief: YAH-HOO.

Again everyone pushes together.

All: YAH-HOO!

Tall Man: We are doing it!

Mother: Now my son won't be able to hide in the sky!

Seventh Chief: YAH-HOO.

Again everyone pushes together.

All: YAH-HOO!

Boy: It will be too high for my arrows to stick into it.

Seventh Chief: YAH-HOO.

Again everyone pushes together.

All: YAH-HOOOO!

First Chief: We have done it!

Narrator: So the sky was pushed up. It was done by everyone working together. That night, when everyone looked overhead, they saw many stars in the sky. The stars were shining through the holes poked into the sky by the poles of everyone who pushed it up higher. No one ever bumped his head on the sky again. And those stars are there to this day.

Meet the Author and Illustrator

Joseph Bruchac writes stories, plays, poems, and articles for children and adults. He is also a storyteller and performs around the country. Joseph is an Abenaki Native American. All of his work centers on keeping alive the Abenaki culture and that of other Native American peoples.

Stefano Vitale grew up in Italy, where he studied art. Stefano especially likes to create pictures on wood. "There is an ancient quality to wood. It has wisdom and age," he says.

Other books written by Joseph Bruchac

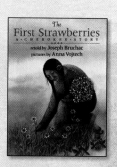

 Find out more about Joseph Bruchac at www.macmillanmh.com

FCAT Author's Purpose

Joseph Bruchac tells a story about people working together. Think about a sport or activity that you do with others. Write a paragraph about how you work together.

212

FCAT Comprehension Check

Retell the Story

Use the Retelling Cards to retell the story.

Retelling Cards

Think and Compare

READ
THINK
EXPLAIN

1. What is the problem in this play? How is the problem solved? Use details and information from the play to support your answers. **Visualize: Problem and Solution**

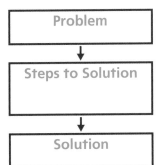

Problem
↓
Steps to Solution
↓
Solution

2. Reread pages 208–209. Why is it important for the people to have a **signal** to push the sky? **Analyze**

3. How have you and your friends or classmates worked together to solve a problem? **Apply**

4. What did you learn from this play about working with others? **Synthesize**

5. How is this play like "Why Sun and Moon Live in the Sky" on pages 196–197? **Reading/Writing Across Texts**

Social Studies

Genre
A Nonfiction Article gives facts about real people, things, or events.

FCAT Text Feature
Interviews are questions asked by one person and answered by another.

Content Vocabulary
author
interviewed
appeal

GETTING TO KNOW JOSEPH BRUCHAC

BY CHRIS LOBACK

Joseph Bruchac is the **author** who wrote *Pushing Up the Sky*. To learn more about Mr. Bruchac, we **interviewed** him. We asked him questions about his work and he answered them. In this interview the words after **Q:** are the question the interviewer asked. The words after **A:** are Joseph Bruchac's answer.

Q: Why do you write Native American stories?

A: I think that they **appeal** to a lot of people. Children and adults have told me that they like to read them. Native American stories are fun to hear and also teach good lessons.

214

Q: Why do you write plays?

A: I write plays for two reasons. The first is that many teachers told me it was hard to find good Native American plays for kids. The second reason is that I love to give kids the chance to take part in a story.

Q: Which of your stories do you like the best?

A: My favorites are the stories with monsters and scary events in them. One of these is *Skeleton Man*. I like this scary story because it shows how even a child can beat a monster if she does the right thing!

FCAT Connect and Compare

1. What is one reason Joseph Bruchac writes plays?
   Interview

2. Think about this interview and *Pushing Up the Sky*. Do you think this is one of Joseph Bruchac's favorite stories? Explain why or why not.
   Reading/Writing Across Texts

RESEARCH INQUIRY **Social Studies Activity**

Find another play by Joseph Bruchac. Perform it with other students.

LOG ON Find more about plays at
www.macmillanmh.com

FCAT **Writer's Craft**

Beginning, Middle, and End
Good writing, even when it is a play, has a clear beginning, middle, and end that keeps to the topic.

Write a Play

 Sun and Wind

by Joe M.

Characters: Narrator, Wind, Sun, Man

Narrator: Wind and Sun were fighting.

Wind: I am stronger than you, Sun.

Sun: No, you're not, Wind. Prove it.

Wind: Do you see that man? Whoever can make him take off his coat is stronger.

Sun: Wind, you can go first.

Man: Brrrr. The wind is cold. I will button up my coat to keep warm.

Wind: I give up. It's your turn, Sun.

Man: The sun is out. Now it is warm. I will take off this heavy coat.

Wind: You win, Sun. You are stronger.

I wrote a strong beginning that tells what this play is about.

My ending shows the end of the action.

216

Writing Prompt

A play includes at least one character that speaks.

Think about characters that you might like to write about.

Write a play with characters speaking to each other.

FCAT Writer's Checklist

✓ **Focus:** My play includes characters that speak to each other

☐ **Organization:** My play includes a good beginning, middle, and end.

✓ **Support:** I include details such as each character's name before he or she speaks.

✓ **Conventions:** I use the correct punctuation, including a colon after each charater's name when he or she speaks.

Talk About It

Why do people
explore new places?

 Find out more about
exploration at
www.macmillanmh.com

EXPLORATION

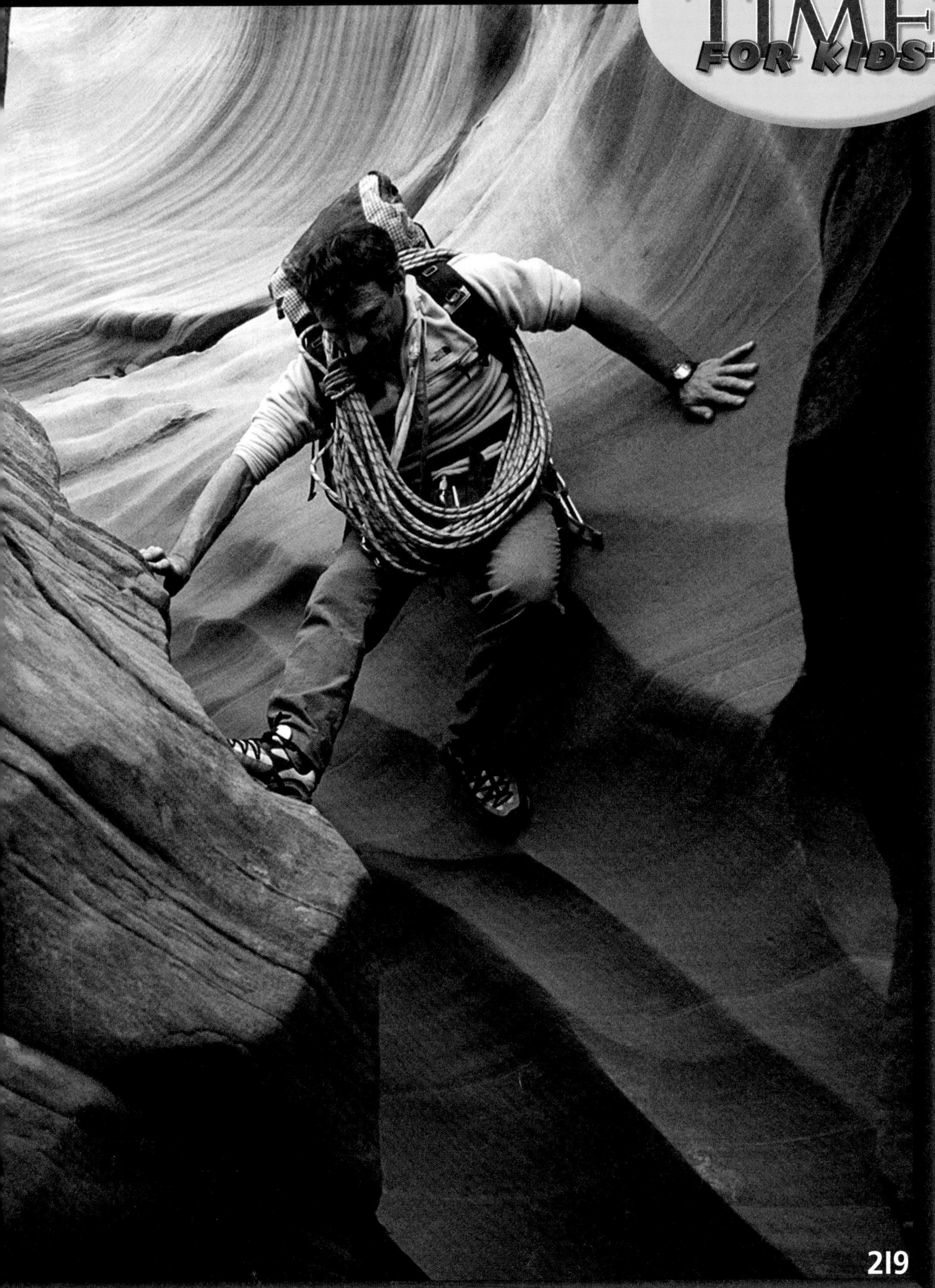

Vocabulary

vast

oceans

areas

voyage

planet

Continents and Oceans

Earth is covered with water and land. There are four **vast** bodies of water called **oceans**. The seven large **areas** of land are called continents.

To visit all of the huge oceans and different continents, you would need to make a **voyage** around the world. A map could help you plan your trip.

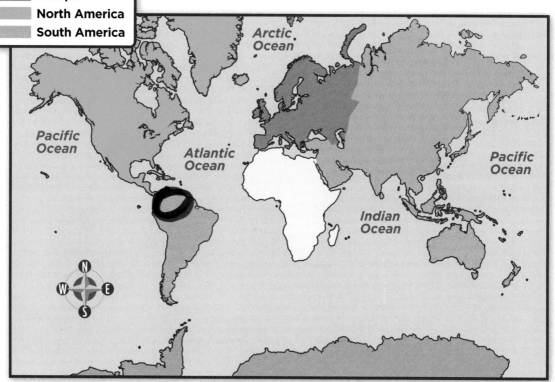

Map Key

- Africa
- Antarctica
- Asia
- Australia
- Europe
- North America
- South America

Arctic Ocean

Pacific Ocean

Atlantic Ocean

Indian Ocean

Pacific Ocean

 Find out more about Earth's continents and oceans at **www.macmillanmh.com**

Record Holders!

How high is the tallest mountain on our **planet**? What is the name of the longest river? Where is the shortest river? If you've ever wondered about Earth's extremes, take a look at these record holders.

RECORD	RECORD HOLDER	THE RECORD
Largest Continent	Asia	17,212,000 square miles
Smallest Continent	Australia	3,132,000 square miles
Highest Mountain	Mount Everest, Asia	29,035 feet
Largest Ocean	Pacific Ocean	60,060,700 square miles
Smallest Ocean	Arctic Ocean	5,427,000 square miles
Longest River	Nile, Africa	4,160 miles
Shortest River	D, North America	120 feet

The Nile flows through ten countries in Africa.

The Arctic Ocean is full of icebergs.

221

Comprehension

Genre

A **Nonfiction Article** gives information about real people, places, and events.

Summarize

Main Ideas and Details

The main idea is what an article is mostly about. Details give more information about the main idea.

Columbus
Explores New Lands

What was Columbus looking for when he set sail across the Atlantic Ocean? What did he find?

Today our **planet** may not seem **vast**. People vacation all over the world. Flying across **oceans** can take just a few hours. But it was a different story 500 years ago.

Christopher Columbus gets ready to sail from Spain.

The date was August 3. The year was 1492. Christopher Columbus was about to make a **voyage** across the Atlantic Ocean. He wanted to find a shorter route from Europe to Asia. Leaving Spain with three ships, he had high hopes for success.

On October 12, Columbus and his crew spotted land. It was an island. Columbus called it San Salvador, and that's what we call it today.

During the next few weeks, Columbus traveled around the islands of the Caribbean Sea. Even though these islands are close to North America, Columbus thought they were off the coast of Asia!

Columbus and his crew celebrated when they spotted land after their long voyage.

The *Santa Maria* (center) was Columbus's largest ship.

In March 1493, Columbus and his crew returned to Spain. But he wasn't finished traveling! He made three more voyages across the Atlantic Ocean, and no two were alike. During his second voyage, he explored other **areas** in the Caribbean. He visited the islands of Dominica, Guadeloupe, Antigua, and Puerto Rico.

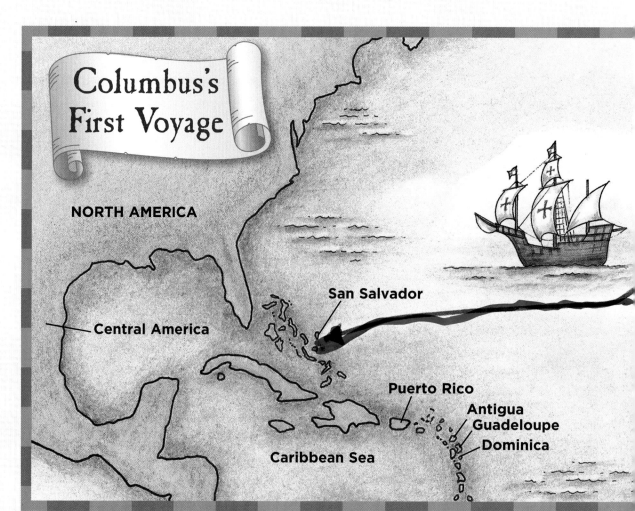

Columbus's First Voyage

NORTH AMERICA

Central America

San Salvador

Puerto Rico

Antigua

Guadeloupe

Dominica

Caribbean Sea

During Columbus's third voyage, in 1498, he landed in South America. By this time he knew he wasn't near Asia. On Columbus's fourth and final voyage, in the early 1500s, he traveled along the coast of Central America.

To remember Columbus's discoveries in the New World, we have a holiday called Columbus Day. On this day we think about how Columbus forever changed life in North and South America.

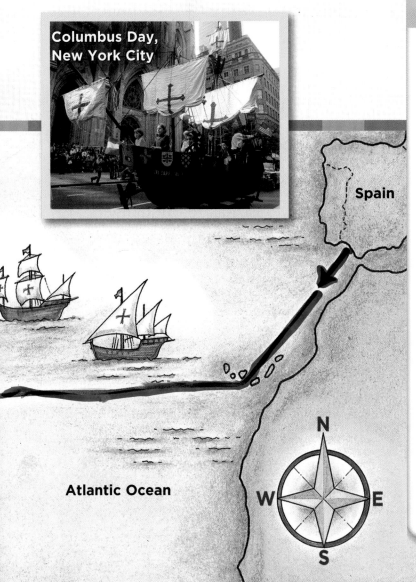

Columbus Day, New York City

Spain

Atlantic Ocean

N W E S

FCAT
Think and Compare

1. What is this selection mostly about?

2. Do you think that Columbus's discoveries were important? Explain why or why not.

3. If you were an explorer, how would you travel— on land, on the sea, or in the air? Why?

4. Which of the places mentioned in this article are continents?

FCAT Test Strategy

Think and Search
Read on to find the answer. Look for clues in more than one place.

Mount Everest

The Roof of the World

Mount Everest is called the "roof of the world." At 29,035 feet, it is the world's highest mountain. It is in the Himalayas, a mountain range in Asia.

Scientists figured out the height of Mount Everest in 1852. Soon many people wanted to climb to the top. It took 101 years for someone to reach that goal. On May 29, 1953, two people reached the "roof of the world." They were Edmund Hillary, from New Zealand, and Tenzing Norgay, a Sherpa climber from Nepal. Sherpas are people who live near Mount Everest.

Climbing Everest has many dangers. There are often avalanches, or snow slides. Climbers can fall into huge cracks in the mountain, called crevasses. Winds may blow at 125 miles per hour. Temperatures may be as cold as 40 degrees below zero. There is less oxygen in the air, making it hard to breathe. People usually climb to the peak only in May and October. Then they miss the winter snows and the summer rains.

Go on ▶

FCAT **Now answer Numbers 1 through 4.**
Base your answers on the article
"The Roof of the World."

1 Mount Everest is

Ⓐ located in America.

Ⓑ the coldest place on Earth.

Ⓒ 101 years old.

Ⓓ a cold, windy mountain in Asia.

2 Why is climbing Mount Everest so
dangerous?

Ⓐ The winds blow at strong levels.

Ⓑ There are avalanches and cold
temperatures.

Ⓒ Nobody has ever done it before.

Ⓓ There are winter snows and fall leaves.

Tip
Look for
Information.

3 What is the main idea of the second paragraph?

Ⓐ Oxygen is thin at the top of the mountain.

Ⓑ Climbing Mount Everest is very hard.

Ⓒ Sherpas live near Mount Everest.

Ⓓ Hillary and Norgay reached the top first.

4 Why is Mount Everest called "the roof of the
world"? Use details and information from the
article to support your answer.

READ
THINK
EXPLAIN

Write to a Prompt

Pablo wrote a paragraph comparing the first climb of Mount Everest to the first trip to the moon.

I made sure that my ideas are clear and organized.

Being First

Being the first to climb to the top of Mount Everest is a lot like the first trip to the moon. The first trip to the moon was very dangerous. So was climbing to the highest place in the world. The astronauts had to ride into space on a rocket. There is no air in space. The astronauts had to take it with them. It is hard to breathe on Mount Everest. Some climbers bring along oxygen to help them breathe. The astronauts had to use special equipment in space. Mountain climbers have to use special climbing tools.

Your Writing Prompt

Now it's your turn to write a paragraph about why you think people set goals that are very hard to reach.

FCAT Some people set difficult goals for themselves.

Think about some goals that are very challenging.

Now write about why you think people set these goals that are very hard to reach.

Writing Hints for Prompts

☑ Think about your purpose for writing.

☑ Plan your writing before beginning.

☑ Make sure your ideas are organized.

☑ Use your best spelling, grammar, and punctuation.

In the Garden

Talk About It

Why do people grow gardens? What is needed to grow a garden?

LOG ON Find out more about gardens at **www.macmillanmh.com**

231

Vocabulary

scent

trade

muscles

prickly

blooming

aroma

FCAT **Context Clues**

Homophones are words that sound the same but have different spellings and different meanings.

Scent and *cent* are homophones.

Scent means smell. A *cent* is money.

City Garden

by Roberto Salazar

When we lived in the country, Dad and I had a garden. We planted beans, peas, and other vegetables. To us, the **scent** of moist soil and growing plants was a kind of perfume. We loved the earthy smell.

Then we moved to the city. We had to **trade** our big country garden for a small city window box.

Cauliflowers

Dad and I missed the garden. So he offered to help my class plant a garden in an empty lot.

First, my class dug up the soil in the lot. We needed strong **muscles** to do all that hard work.

Next, we planted seeds and small plants in neat rows. We wore gloves because some plants had sharp **prickly** thorns.

Soon the flowers were **blooming**. The lot reminded me of my old garden. It was great to smell the fresh **aroma** of plants that filled the air. Then, tiny vegetables grew. Last, the vegetables became large and ripe, so we picked them. Dad and I enjoyed some tasty vegetables from our city garden.

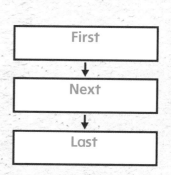

Reread for **Comprehension**

Summarize
FCAT Retell Events in Order

You can summarize an article by **retelling the events in order,** or telling what happened first, next, and last. Reread the article and use the chart to understand the order of the important events in it, or what happened first, next, and last.

First
↓
Next
↓
Last

Comprehension

Genre
Realistic Fiction is a made-up story that could happen in real life.

Summarize

Retell Events in Order
As you read the story, use the **Retelling** Chart.

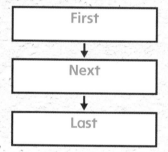

First

↓

Next

↓

Last

Read to Find Out
How does the garden change from the beginning to the end of the story?

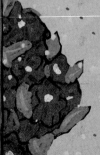

The Ugly Vegetables

by Grace Lin

In the spring I helped my mother start our garden.
We used tall shovels to turn the grass upside down,
and I saw pink worms wriggle around. It was hard work.
When we stopped to rest, we saw that the neighbors
were starting their gardens too.

"Hello, Irma!" my mother called to Mrs. Crumerine.
Mrs. Crumerine was digging too. She was using a small
shovel, one that fit in her hand.

"Mommy," I asked, "why are we using such big
shovels? Mrs. Crumerine has a small one."

"Because our garden needs more digging," she said.

I helped my mother plant the seeds, and we dragged the hose to the garden. "Hi, Linda! Hi, Mickey!" I called to the Fitzgeralds. They were sprinkling water on their garden with green watering cans.

"Mommy," I asked, "why are we using a hose? Linda and Mickey use watering cans."

"Because our garden needs more water," she said.

Then my mother drew funny pictures on pieces of
paper, and I stuck them into the garden.

"Hello, Roseanne!" my mother called across the street
to Mrs. Angelhowe.

"Mommy," I asked, "why are we sticking these papers
in the garden? Mrs. Angelhowe has seed packages in
her garden."

"Because our garden is going to grow Chinese vegetables,"
she told me. "These are the names of the vegetables in
Chinese, so I can tell which plants are growing where."

One day I saw our garden growing. Little green stems
that looked like grass had popped out from the ground.

"Our garden's growing!" I yelled. "Our garden's growing!"

I rushed over to the neighbors' gardens to see if theirs
had grown. Their plants looked like little leaves.

"Mommy," I asked, "why do our plants look like grass?
The neighbors' plants look different."

"Because they are growing flowers," she said.

"Why can't we grow flowers?" I asked.

"These are better than flowers," she said.

239

Soon all the neighbors' gardens were **blooming**.
Up and down the street grew rainbows of flowers.

The wind always smelled sweet, and butterflies
and bees flew everywhere. Everyone's garden was
beautiful, except for ours.

Ours was all dark green and ugly.

"Why didn't we grow flowers?" I asked again.

"These are better than flowers," Mommy said again.

I looked, but saw only black-purple-green vines, fuzzy wrinkled leaves, **prickly** stems, and a few little yellow flowers.

"I don't think so," I said.

"You wait and see," Mommy said.

Before long, our vegetables grew. Some were big and lumpy. Some were thin and green and covered with bumps. Some were just plain icky yellow. They were ugly vegetables.

FCAT Retell Events in Order
Describe how the garden changes from the beginning of the story until this point.

Sometimes I would go over to the neighbors' and look
at their pretty gardens. They would show the poppies and
peonies and petunias to me, and I would feel sad that our
garden wasn't as nice.

One day my mother and I picked the vegetables from
the garden. We filled a whole wheelbarrow full of them.
We wheeled them to the kitchen. My mother washed
them and took a big knife and started to chop them.

"Aie-yow!" she said when she cut them. She had to use all her **muscles**. The vegetables were hard and tough.

"This is a sheau hwang gua," Mommy said, handing me a bumpy, curled vegetable. She pointed at the other vegetables. "This is shiann tsay. That's a torng hau."

FCAT Retell Events in Order

What steps does the girl's mother take to prepare the vegetables?

I went outside to play. While I was playing catch with Mickey, a magical **aroma** filled the air. I saw the neighbors standing on their porches with their eyes closed, smelling the sky. They took deep breaths of air, like they were trying to eat the smell.

The wind carried it up and down the street.
Even the bees and the butterflies seemed to smell
the **scent** in the breeze.

I smelled it too. It made me hungry, and it was
coming from my house!

When I followed it to my house, my mother was putting a big bowl of soup on the table. The soup was yellow and red and green and pink.

"This is a special soup," Mommy said, and she smiled.

She gave me a small bowl full of it and I tasted it. It was so good! The flavors of the soup seemed to dance in my mouth and laugh all the way down to my stomach. I smiled.

"Do you like it?" Mommy asked me.

I nodded and held out my bowl for some more.

"It's made from our vegetables," she told me.

Then the doorbell rang, and we ran to open the door.

All our neighbors were standing at the door
holding flowers.

"We noticed you were cooking." Mr. Fitzgerald
laughed as he held out his flowers. "And we thought
maybe you might be interested in a **trade**!"

We laughed too, and my mother gave them each
their own bowl of her special soup.

252

My mother told them what each vegetable was
and how she grew it. She gave them the soup recipe
and put some soup into jars for them to take home.
I ate five bowls of soup.

It was the best dinner ever.

The next spring, when my mother was starting her garden, we planted some flowers next to the Chinese vegetables. Mrs. Crumerine, the Fitzgeralds, and the Angelhowes planted some Chinese vegetables next to their flowers.

Soon the whole neighborhood was growing Chinese vegetables in their gardens. Up and down the street, little green plants poked out of the ground. Some looked like leaves and some looked like grass, and when the flowers started blooming, you could smell soup in the air.

In the Garden with Grace Lin

As a girl, **Grace Lin** wanted to be an ice skater. She drew many pictures of herself skating. But when Grace tried to skate, she often fell on her face. Then she looked at the pictures she had drawn. "Maybe I'll be an artist," Grace thought.

Grace says that *The Ugly Vegetables* is based on her childhood. "My mother used to grow Chinese vegetables in her garden while all the neighbors grew flowers. Year after year, I looked with disgust at our ugly garden and asked, 'Why can't we grow flowers?' My mother always answered, 'Because these are better than flowers.' I never agreed, until one day . . ."

Other books written and illustrated by Grace Lin

LOG ON Find out more about Grace Lin at **www.macmillanmh.com**

FCAT Author's Purpose

Grace Lin tells a story about how she changed her mind about something. Think about a time when you had strong ideas about something and then changed your mind. Write about the event and why it was important to you.

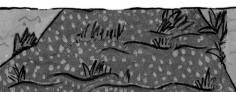

 Comprehension Check

Retell the Story

Use the Retelling Cards to retell the story.

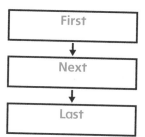

Retelling Cards

Think and Compare

READ
THINK
EXPLAIN

1. Describe in order how the girl and her mother care for the garden. Use information and details from the story to support your answer. **Summarize: Retell Events in Order**

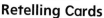

First

↓

Next

↓

Last

2. Reread page 244. How does the girl feel about her vegetable garden? Why? **Evaluate**

3. What would you like to have **blooming** in a garden—flowers or vegetables? Why? **Synthesize**

4. Why is it important for people to learn about different cultures? **Analyze**

5. Why might the boy in "City Garden," on pages 232–233, like the garden in *The Ugly Vegetables*? Explain. **Reading/Writing Across Texts**

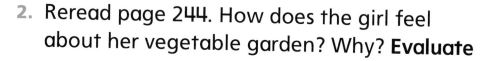

Genre
Nonfiction gives information and facts about a topic.

FCAT ## Text Feature
Written Directions are steps that tell you how to make or do something.

Content Vocabulary
soil

pottery

directions

Florida Gardens

Did you know that dirt is not just dirt? Florida has different kinds of dirt, or **soil**. These soils are used for different things.

Some Florida soil contains clay. People use one type of Florida clay to make **pottery**. Other soil contains rock. One kind of rock, limestone, is used to make roads and buildings. People make cement from this rock. Another kind of rock is phosphate rock. Phosphate rock is made into plant food that can be added to the soil in gardens.

Limestone

Phosphate Rock

Clay

Some flowers are grown in soil that is mostly sand and shell.

You can grow many kinds of plants in Florida. Different plants grow in different parts of the state. They grow in different types of soil.

Along the coast, the soil is mostly sand and shell. A few grasses and flowers grow here. In other places, the soil is a mixture of sand and other materials. Many kinds of plants and trees grow in these areas. People grow fruit and nut trees in these soils. They grow flowers and vegetables, too.

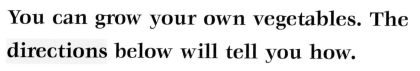

You can grow your own vegetables. The directions below will tell you how.

1 Talk to another gardener, or someone at a local nursery. Find out which vegetables grow best where you live. Find out when a good time to plant seeds is.

2 Dig up the soil where you will plant. Pull out the weeds. Remove any rocks.

3 Rake the soil flat.

4. Poke small holes in the soil. Put a seed in each hole. Cover the seeds with soil.

5. Water the seeds.

6. Check your garden every day.

7. Water the soil when it starts to dry out. Pull out any weeds.

8. Pick the ripe vegetables. Enjoy!

FCAT Connect and Compare

1. When you are planting a garden, what do you do right after you put a seed in each hole? **Written Directions**

2. Think about this article and *The Ugly Vegetables*. What kind of vegetables would you like to grow? How would you plant these vegetables? **Reading/Writing Across Texts**

Science Activity

Research a vegetable you like. Write a paragraph telling what kind of soil and climate that vegetable needs to grow.

Find more vegetable facts at
www.macmillanmh.com

FCAT Writer's Craft

Precise Words
Good writers use **precise words** to help make their writing clear and to convey the correct meaning.

> I use precise word to tell where we were.

> These words tell exactly what I have.

The Garden Project
by Lydia P.

Mom and I were in the kitchen talking when I remembered my science project. "Oh no! I need an idea for my *science project*," I told her. "It's due tomorrow!"

"Why don't you think about it while you water the garden," Mom said.

A little while later I came back inside. "I have my idea all *set*," I said. Then I showed her the seeds that were left over from planting our garden. "I'm going to show different types of seeds and the plants they grow into. I got my idea from the garden!"

Writing Prompt

Families can be good subjects for stories.

Think about a real or make-believe family.

Now, write a story about this family.

FCAT Writer's Checklist

✓ **Focus:** My writing clearly presents a story about a family.

✓ **Organization:** My writing has a clear beginning, middle, and end.

☑ **Support:** I use detailed, precise words to make my writing clear.

✓ **Conventions:** My sentences are complete. I use capital letters in all the right places.

OUR MOON

Talk About It

What do you know about the moon? Does it always look the same?

LOG ON Find out more about the moon at **www.macmillanmh.com**

Discover the Moon

Scientists have **discovered** many things about the moon. They have learned about it by observing and by visiting the moon.

Scientists know that the moon does not give off its own light. Its **visible** light, the light you can see from Earth, is from the sun shining on it.

Scientists have learned that the moon takes about 28 days to move around Earth. As the moon moves, only some of the moon's bright surface is visible from Earth. These changes in the way the moon looks are called **lunar**, or moon, phases.

This picture shows all the different phases of the moon.

In 1969 scientists learned a lot more about the moon when a spacecraft flew and landed there. The vehicle carried three astronauts. These people walked on the moon's rocky surface. With each step they took, they left a mark, or footprint, in the gray dust. The astronauts found out that the moon is made of mostly rock.

Reread for **Comprehension**

Summarize
FCAT Compare and Contrast

When you summarize, you can **compare and contrast** information that you read about. You think about how things are alike and different. Reread the selection and use the chart to compare and contrast facts about the moon and Earth.

Earth	Moon

267

Comprehension

Genre
Nonfiction gives information and facts about a topic.

Summarize
Compare and Contrast As you read, use your Compare and Contrast Chart.

Earth	Moon
Earth is the only planet with people.	The Moon is not a planet it is a huge star in space.

Read to Find Out
What information do you learn about the moon?

Award
Winning
Author

THE MOON
SEYMOUR SIMON

The moon is Earth's closest neighbor in space. It is about one quarter of a million miles away. In space that is very close.

The moon travels around Earth. It is Earth's only natural satellite. A satellite is an object that travels around another object. The moon takes about twenty-seven days and eight hours to go around the Earth once.

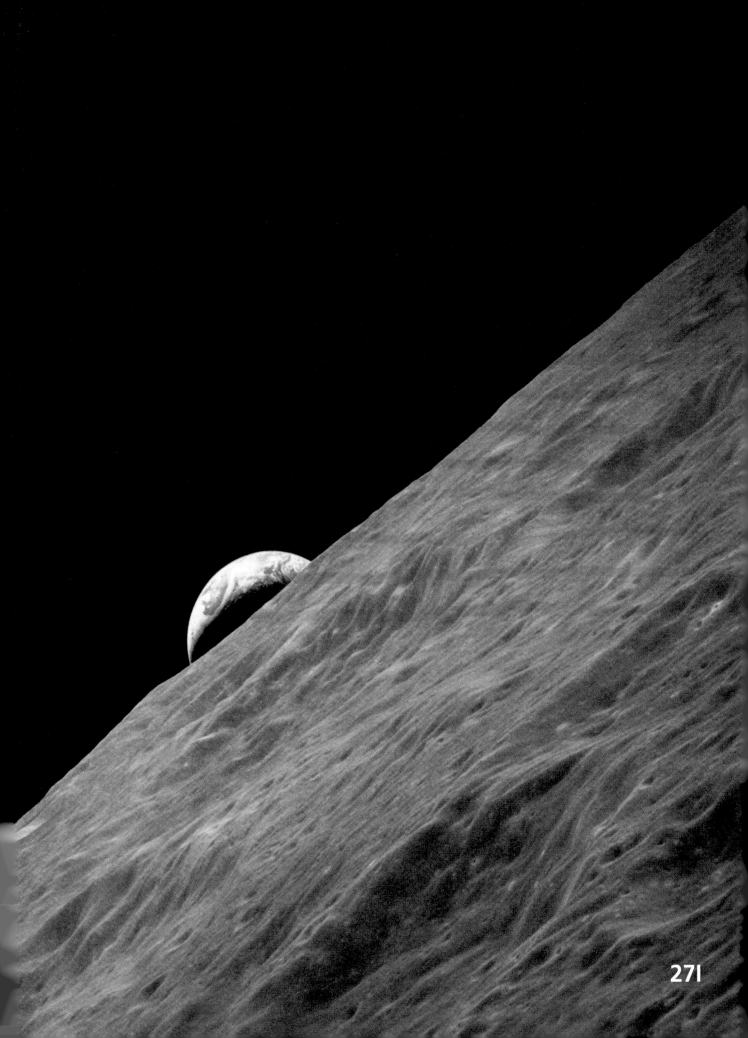

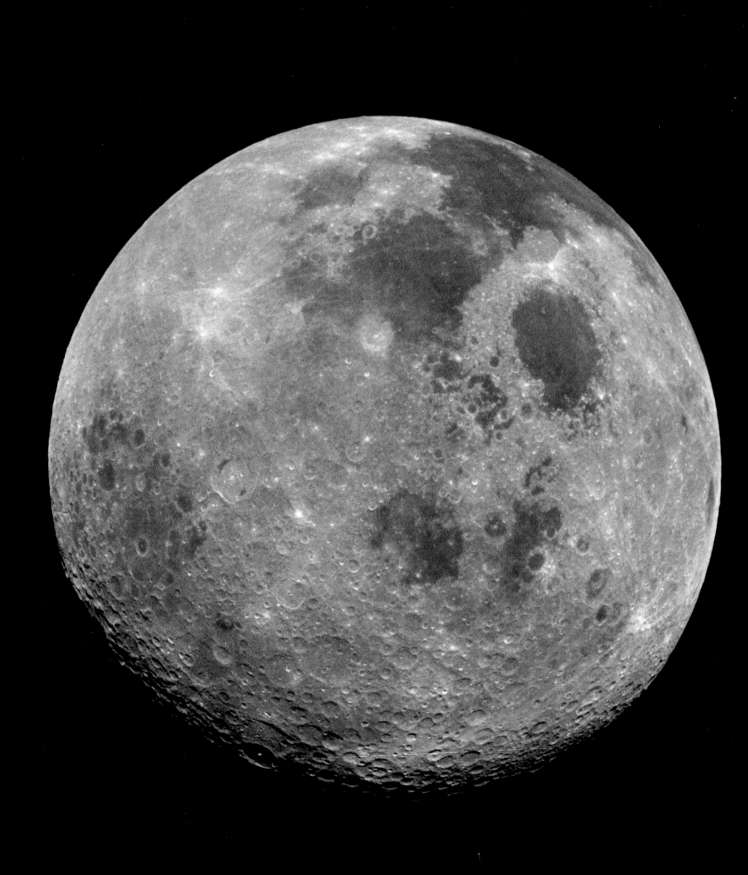

The moon is so close to the Earth that you can easily see light and dark on its **surface**. This photograph of the moon was taken through a telescope on Earth. The light places are mostly mountains and hills. The dark places are flatlands.

FCAT Compare and Contrast
What types of places can be found on the moon's surface?

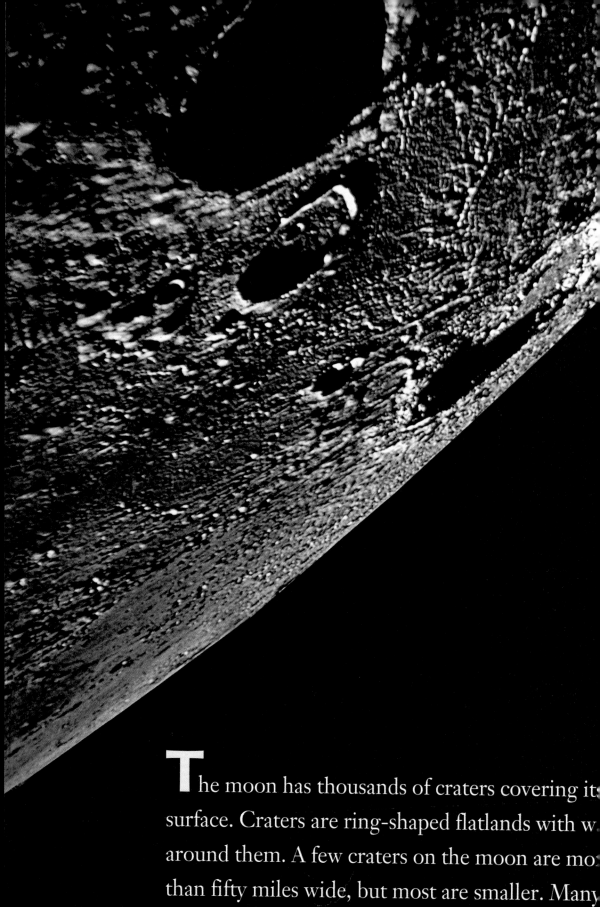

The moon has thousands of craters covering its surface. Craters are ring-shaped flatlands with w around them. A few craters on the moon are mo than fifty miles wide, but most are smaller. Many the craters are only a few feet wide.

274

The moon is made of rock. We can see only part of the moon lit by sunlight. Sometimes we see the full moon. Other times we see a thin sliver. Every night the moon looks a little different. Each different shape is called a phase of the moon. The phases go from all-dark (new moon) through full moon, and back to new moon in about twenty-nine days. We call the phase in this photograph a crescent moon.

From earliest times, people gazed up at the moon and wondered about it. Were there living things on the moon? Would we ever be able to travel to the moon?

In 1961, the United States government decided to try to send a person to the moon within ten years.

The space program was named Apollo. This photograph taken from the Apollo 11 *Columbia* **spacecraft** shows the **lunar** landing ship *Eagle*. It is on its way back from the surface of the moon. The surface of the moon is **visible** sixty miles below the spacecraft. A partly lit Earth hangs above the moon's horizon.

277

On July 20, 1969, Neil Armstrong became the first person to set foot on the moon. Armstrong was one of the astronauts on the Apollo 11 flight to the moon. He was followed shortly by Edwin Aldrin, another member of the United States Apollo 11 space flight. This is a photograph of Astronaut Aldrin standing on the moon. The face mask of his space suit reflects Astronaut Armstrong.

This **footprint** on the moon marks the first time that human beings have walked on ground that was not Earth. The footprint may last for a million years or longer. That is because there is no air on the moon and without air, there can be no winds to blow dust around.

The astronauts **discovered** that the moon is a silent, strange place. The moon has no air. Air carries sound. With no air, the moon is completely silent. Even when the astronauts broke rocks or used the rockets on their spaceship, sound could not be heard.

The sky on the moon is always black. On Earth, we can see stars only at night. On the moon, stars shine all the time.

FCAT Compare and Contrast
Why do you think the moon is described as a "silent, strange place"? Explain how this is different from Earth.

The moon does not have air, water, clouds, rain, or snow. It does not have weather. But the surface of the moon does warm up and cool off. The ground gets very hot or very cold because there is no air to spread the heat.

The temperatures in the daytime can be above the boiling point of water. At night, the temperature can drop hundreds of degrees below zero. The astronauts' space suits kept their bodies at the right temperature. The astronauts carried tanks on their backs that contained the air they needed for breathing.

Each Apollo crew brought back more information about the moon. Scientists all over the world studied the information the astronauts brought back. They learned that the moon is about the same age as Earth. But the moon's soil and rocks are different from Earth's. For instance, moon rocks contain no water at all, while almost all rocks on Earth contain a small amount of water.

Apollo 17 was the last spaceship to carry people to the moon. It was launched in December 1972. The astronauts of Apollo 17 discovered the oldest rock ever found on the moon. Before the astronauts returned to Earth, they left a plaque on the moon showing the history of moon travel.

Earth and its moon are close in space, but very different from each other. Earth is a blue, cloud-covered planet, filled with living things. The moon is a dead world. Without air or water, a cloud can never appear in its black sky and a raindrop will never fall.

FIND OUT ABOUT SEYMOUR AND SPACE

The very first piece **SEYMOUR SIMON** wrote for children was an article about the moon. He remembers, "I submitted an article, before we set foot on the moon, about what we might find there."

Seymour was always interested in science and space. In junior high school he joined a space club. "During that time," Seymour says, "I made my own telescope. I met astronomers. And that interest in space led to the many books about space that I have written and still write: books about the planets and books about stars and the sun, and news from space."

Other books written by Seymour Simon

 Find out more about Seymour Simon at **www.macmillanmh.com**

FCAT ## Author's Purpose

Seymour Simon teaches his readers about the moon. Write about a science topic that you like. Explain why you like it.

FCAT Comprehension Check

Retell the Story

Use the Retelling Cards to retell the selection.

Retelling Cards

Think and Compare

READ THINK EXPLAIN

1. How is the moon the same as and different from the Earth? Use details and information from the selection to explain your answer.
Summarize: Compare and Contrast

Earth	Moon

2. Reread page 283. Why did the astronauts wear space suits when they walked on the moon's **surface**? **Analyze**

3. Why would you might want to travel into space? **Synthesize**

4. Why do people think it is important to learn more about the moon? **Evaluate**

5. What did you learn from "Discover the Moon" on pages 266–267 that you did not learn from *The Moon*? **Reading/Writing Across Texts**

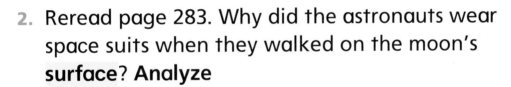

Poetry

Genre
Poems can describe something and help you form a picture of it in your mind.

Literary Elements
Personification is a way of speaking about a thing as if it were human and could do things that humans do.

Imagery is a poet's use of words to create a picture in the reader's mind.

Night Comes...

by Beatrice Schenk de Regniers

Night comes
leaking
out of the sky.

Stars come
peeking.

Moon comes
sneaking,
silvery-sly.

Who is
shaking,
shivery-
quaking?

Who is afraid
of the night?

Not I.

FCAT Connect and Compare

1. How does the poet use personification in this poem? **Personification**

2. Think about how the moon is described in *The Moon* and how it is described in this poem. Why are the descriptions so different? **Reading/Writing Across Texts**

 Find out more about the sky at **www.macmillanmh.com**

Write About an Imaginary Place

A Good Paragraph
A paragraph is a group of sentences that forms a unit with a central idea. In a good paragraph, details support the main idea.

My Moon Home

by Trevor S.

This paragraph is about my home on the moon.

My new home on the moon is very different from my home on Earth. On Earth, our house had lots of big rooms. Here, my parents and I share a small pod. Ten round pods make up each living complex. The complex is filled with other families.

This paragraph has more details about our pod.

Our pod doesn't have a kitchen. We don't need one because we just heat up plastic packets of food. Astronauts deliver our food in big shipments every six months.

Writing Prompt

An imaginary place is made up, or not from real life.

Think about an imaginary place that you make up.

Now, write about an imaginary place.

FCAT Writer's Checklist

✓ **Focus:** My writing clearly presents an imaginary place.

✓ **Organization:** I write good paragraphs, each with a central idea.

✓ **Support:** I include details that support the main or central idea of each paragraph.

✓ **Conventions:** I vary my sentences so that they flow. I use the correct punctuation.

FCAT

Review

Author's Purpose
Problem and Solution
Compare and Contrast
Captions
Diagrams and Labels
Compound Words

A Birthday Treat

Mom   Dad   Jessie

Jessie's friends

Mom: We are going to the science museum for your birthday today!

Jessie: Hooray! That's my favorite place! Can I invite my friends Ashley, Samantha, and Blake to go with me, please?

Mom: I'm sorry, but I only have two tickets. Also, we need to leave right away. We don't want to miss the volcano movie. Seat belt on? Good. Do you remember where the museum is?

Jessie: Yes. Make a left onto Elm Street. Make a right at the gas station onto Pine Street. The museum is on the right.

Mom: We have 45 minutes before the movie starts. Do you want to look around?

Jessie: Sure! Let's check out the dinosaur exhibit. The dinosaur skeletons reach to the ceiling!

Mom: Before we go, I need to stop at the cafeteria. Let's open the door.

Jessie: What's this?

Jessie's friends: Surprise! Happy birthday!

Mom and Dad: Surprise!

Jessie: Wow! What a great birthday treat!

The Invention of Hook-and-Loop Tape

Did you ever wonder how inventors come up with their ideas? Do they study something closely? Do they work with partners? Or do ideas come to them by accident?

Inventions may begin in any of these ways. Or, they may be the result of them all. That's how it happened for George de Mestral. His invention is hook-and-loop tape. That's the sticky fabric tape that fastens sneakers, caps, and backpacks.

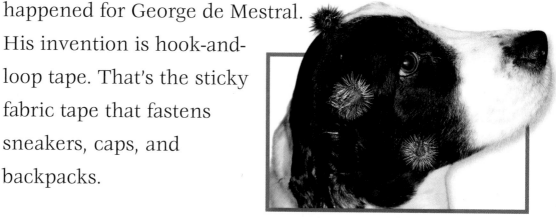

The prickly bur is a seedpod of the burdock plant.

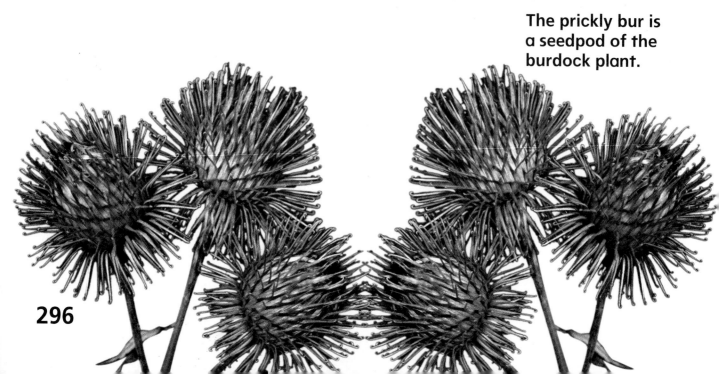

296

George's idea began when he returned from a walk with his dog. Burs were stuck to his pants and his dog's fur. George pulled them off, but wondered how they held on.

George began to study the burs. What if he could discover the secret of their strong grip? Maybe he could invent a strong fastener.

George's breakthrough came with a microscope. He saw that burs were covered with tiny hooks. The hooks grabbed onto anything with a loop!

Next, George worked with a weaver to make one piece of tape with hooks, the other piece with loops. Put together, they imitated a bur.

Today people use hook-and-loop tape instead of buttons, strings, or zippers.

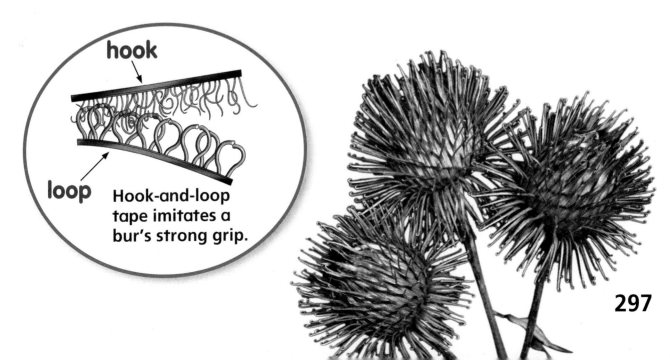

hook

loop

Hook-and-loop tape imitates a bur's strong grip.

Count on a Celebration

Talk About It

What kinds of celebrations does your family have? Do you have special traditions?

LOG ON Find out more about celebrations at **www.macmillanmh.com**

Bobo's Celebration

by Keith Fish

Mom and I planned a surprise party for my brother Bobo.

First, my mom and I made a **menu**. It listed all the foods we would serve. The main dish was Bobo's favorite— seaweed stew!

Mom asked me to **fetch** the things we needed, so I swam to the Ship Shop. When I went to pay, I knew that I was **forgetting** something. I checked my list. I had not remembered the seaweed! So, I asked Ron Ray if he had any.

"Yes, I have some seaweed," he said. "That's 20 sand dollars, please." I paid him and swam home.

The day of the party, the stew **simmered** on the stove. I watched it bubble over low heat for hours.

An hour before the party, the guests **assembled** in one spot. The group gathered with Mom and me by the reef. When Bobo came, we yelled "Surprise!"

Bobo's party was fun. We **devoured** all of the stew. We ate until there was nothing left. Bobo said it was the best surprise ever!

Reread for **Comprehension**

Story Structure

FCAT **Compare Fantasy and Reality**

A **fantasy** story could not happen in real life. A **reality** story could happen. Reread the story and use the chart to figure out whether "Bobo's Celebration" is a fantasy or reality story.

Reality	Fantasy
What Could Happen?	What Could Not Happen?

Comprehension

Genre

Fantasy has made-up characters and settings that could not happen in real life.

Story Structure

FCAT **Compare Fantasy and Reality**

As you read, use your **Fantasy and Reality** Chart.

Reality	Fantasy
What Could Happen?	What Could Not Happen?

Read to Find Out

What do the mice do in this story that they can't do in real life?

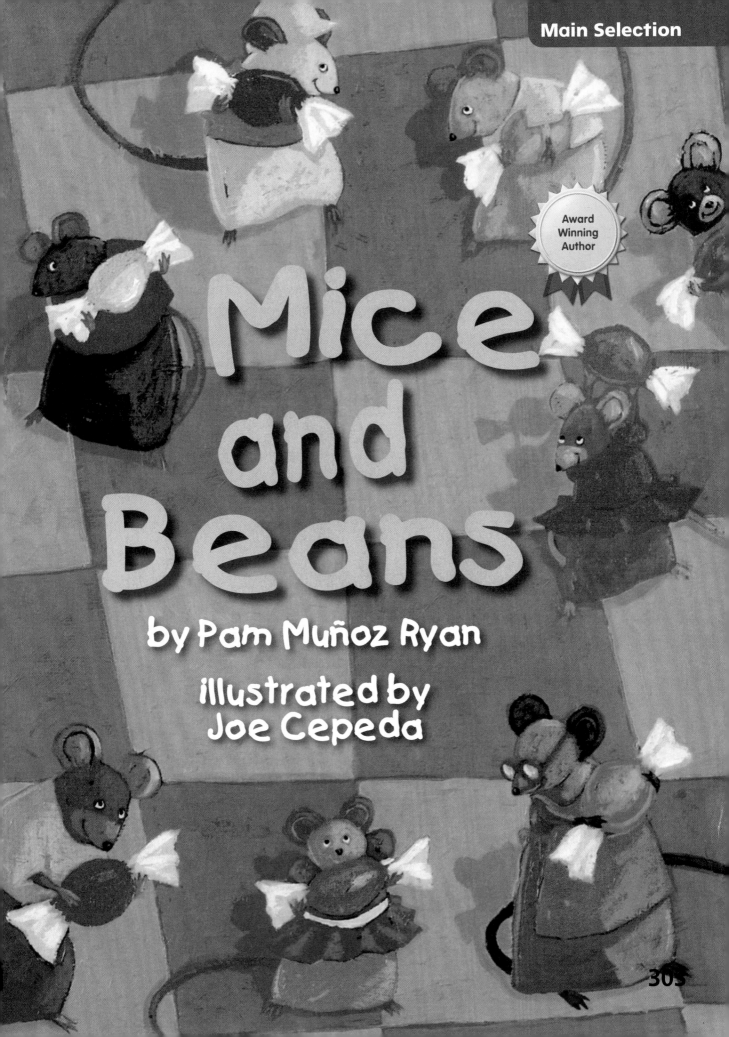

Award Winning Author

Mice and Beans

by Pam Muñoz Ryan

illustrated by
Joe Cepeda

Rosa María lived in a tiny house with a tiny yard. But she had a big heart, a big family, and more than anything, she loved to cook big meals for them.

In one week, her youngest grandchild, Little Catalina, would be seven years old, and the whole family would squeeze into her *casita* for the party.

Rosa María didn't mind because she believed what her mother had always said: "When there's room in the heart, there's room in the house, **except** for a mouse."

Sunday, Rosa María planned the **menu**: *enchiladas*, rice and beans (no dinner was complete without rice and beans!), birthday cake, lemonade, and a *piñata* filled with candy.

She ordered the birthday present—something Little Catalina had wanted for a long time.

Satisfied with the plans, she wiped down the table so she wouldn't get mice and took out a mousetrap just in case. She was sure she had set one the night before, but now she couldn't find it. Maybe she'd forgotten.

When it was set and ready to **snap,** she turned off the light and went to bed.

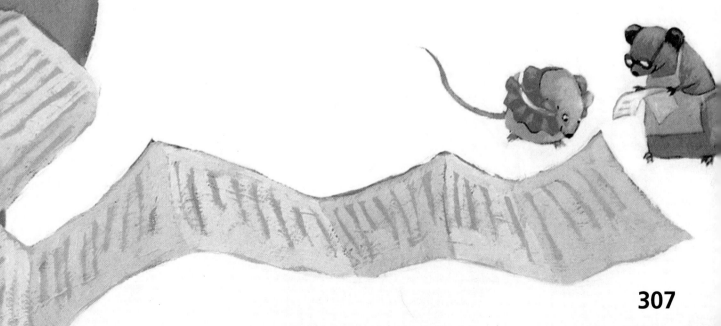

Monday, Rosa María did the laundry. She washed and ironed her largest tablecloth and the twenty-four napkins that matched. But when she finished, she only counted twenty-three.

"*No importa,*" she said. "It doesn't matter. So what if someone has a napkin that doesn't match? The important thing is that we're all together."

After dinner she swept the floor and checked the mousetrap.

But it was missing.

Didn't I set one last night? she wondered.

She hurried to the cupboard to **fetch** another, and when it was set and ready to **snap,** she turned off the light and went to bed.

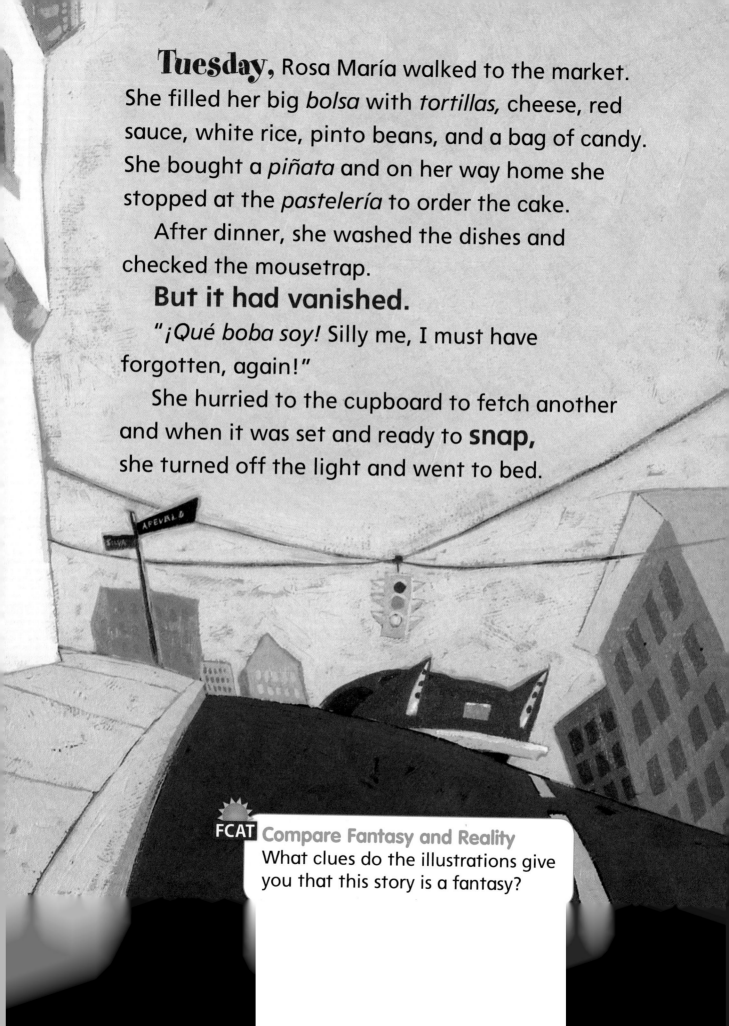

Tuesday, Rosa María walked to the market. She filled her big *bolsa* with *tortillas,* cheese, red sauce, white rice, pinto beans, and a bag of candy. She bought a *piñata* and on her way home she stopped at the *pastelería* to order the cake.

After dinner, she washed the dishes and checked the mousetrap.

But it had vanished.

"*¡Qué boba soy!* Silly me, I must have forgotten, again!"

She hurried to the cupboard to fetch another and when it was set and ready to **snap,** she turned off the light and went to bed.

FCAT Compare Fantasy and Reality
What clues do the illustrations give you that this story is a fantasy?

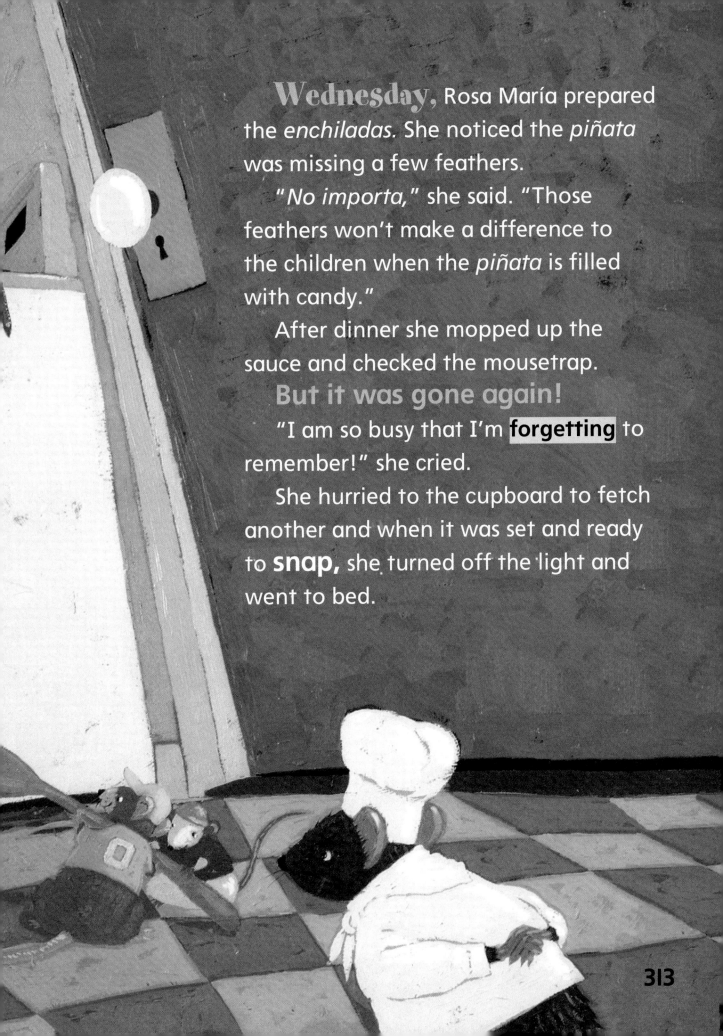

Wednesday, Rosa María prepared the *enchiladas*. She noticed the *piñata* was missing a few feathers.

"*No importa,*" she said. "Those feathers won't make a difference to the children when the *piñata* is filled with candy."

After dinner she mopped up the sauce and checked the mousetrap. **But it was gone again!**

"I am so busy that I'm **forgetting** to remember!" she cried.

She hurried to the cupboard to fetch another and when it was set and ready to **snap,** she turned off the light and went to bed.

Thursday, Rosa María simmered the beans. She searched for her favorite wooden spoon, the one she always used to cook *frijoles,* but she couldn't find it.

"*No importa,*" she said. "The beans will taste just as good if I use another spoon."

She added water all day long until the beans were plump and soft. Then she scrubbed the stove and checked the mousetrap.

But it was nowhere in sight!

"*¡Cielos!*" she said. "Heavens! Where is my mind?"

She hurried to the cupboard to fetch another and when it was set and ready to **snap,** she turned off the light and went to bed.

Friday, Rosa María picked up the cake and seven candles.

Tomorrow was the big day. Rosa María knew she mustn't forget anything, so she carefully went over the list one last time.

After dinner she wrapped the cake and checked the mousetrap.

She couldn't believe her eyes.

No mousetrap!

"Thank goodness I've got plenty."

She hurried to the cupboard to fetch another and when it was set and ready to **snap,** she turned off the light and went to bed.

Saturday, Rosa María cooked the rice. As the workers **assembled** Little Catalina's present, she set the table and squeezed the juiciest lemons from her tree.

"Let's see," she said, feeling very proud. "*Enchiladas,* rice and beans (no dinner was complete without rice and beans!), birthday cake, and lemonade. I know I have forgotten something, but what? **The candles!**"

But she only counted six.

"*No importa,*" she said. "I will arrange the six candles in the shape of a seven and Little Catalina will be just as happy. **Now,** everything is ready."

But WAS everything ready?

FCAT **Compare Fantasy and Reality**
How do you think the problem will be solved? Could this happen in real life?

That afternoon Rosa María's family filled her tiny *casita*. They ate the *enchiladas* and rice and beans. They drank the fresh-squeezed lemonade. And they **devoured** the cake.

Little Catalina loved her present—a swing set! And after every cousin had a turn, they chanted, "*¡La piñata! ¡La piñata!*"

They ran to the walnut tree and threw a rope over a high branch.

Whack! Whack! Little Catalina swung the *piñata* stick.

"Wait!" cried Rosa María as she remembered what she'd forgotten. But it was too late.

Crack! The *piñata* separated, and the children scrambled to collect the candy.

How could that be? Rosa María puzzled.
I must have filled it without even realizing!
She laughed at her own forgetfulness
as she hugged her granddaughter and
said, *"Feliz cumpleaños,* my Little Catalina.
Happy birthday."

325

After everyone had gone, Rosa María tidied her kitchen and thought contentedly about the *fiesta*. She pictured the happy look on Little Catalina's face when the candy spilled from the *piñata*. But Rosa María still couldn't remember when she had filled it.

"*No importa,*" she said. "It was a wonderful day."

But as Rosa María swept out the cupboard, she discovered the telltale signs of mice!

"*¡Ratones!*" she cried. "Where are my mousetraps? I will set them all!"

She inched to the floor and when she did, something caught her eye.

She looked closer.

Maybe I **didn't** fill the *piñata,* she thought.

"Was it possible?" she asked, shaking her head. "Could I have had help?"

Rosa María looked at the leftovers. Too much for one person.

And what was it her mother had always said? "When there's room in the heart, there's room in the house . . . **even** for a mouse."

"*¡Fíjate!* Imagine that!" she said. "I remembered the words wrong all these years."

Besides, how many could there be? Two? Four?

"*No importa,*" she said. "It doesn't matter if a few helpful mice live here, too."

Then she turned off the light and went to bed . . .

. . . and
never set
another
mousetrap
again.

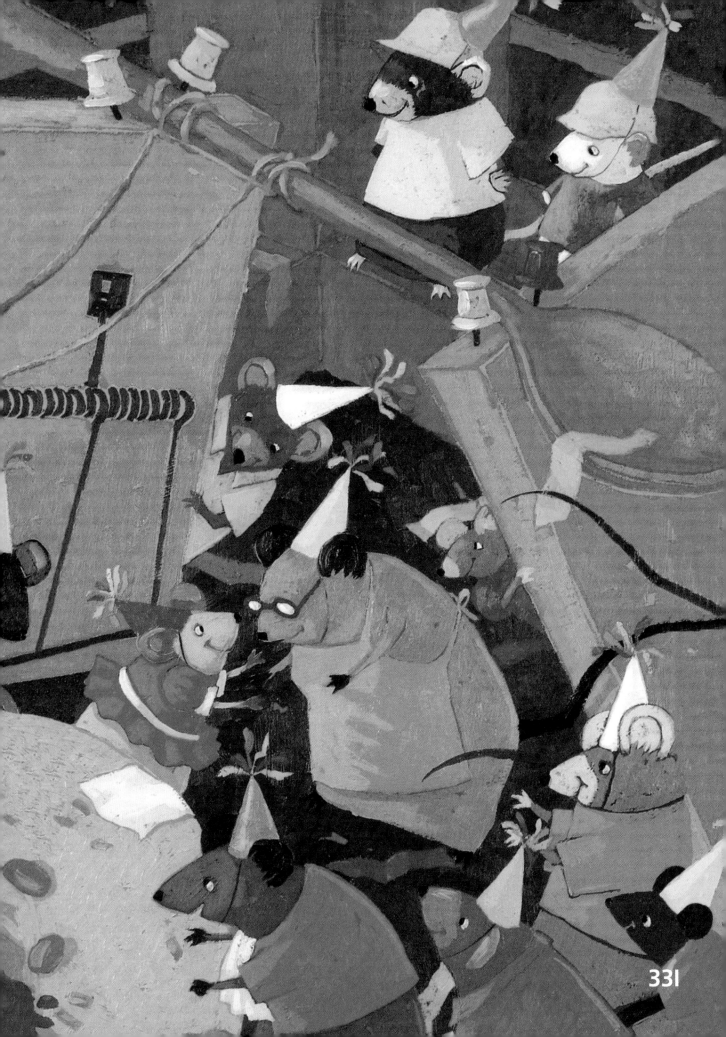

Celebrating with Joe Cepeda

Joe Cepeda says that many parties from his childhood looked just like the one in this book. For his son's parties, Joe always finds a special piñata. He has even made a hand-painted piñata stick. He hopes it will become a part of their family traditions.

Joe has received many awards for *Mice and Beans*. He has illustrated more than 15 other children's books. He also does artwork for magazines, newspapers, and businesses.

Other books illustrated by Joe Cepeda

LOG ON Find out more about Joe Cepeda at **www.macmillanmh.com**

FCAT Author's Purpose

Joe Cepeda shares what he knows about parties. What traditions do you share in your family? What are some things your family does together? Write a paragraph about one of them.

332

 FCAT Comprehension Check

Retell the Story

Use the Retelling Cards to retell the story.

Retelling Cards

Think and Compare

1. Which parts of this story could happen in real life? Which could not? Use details and information from the story to support your answer. **Story Structure: Compare Fantasy and Reality**

Reality	Fantasy
What Could Happen?	What Could Not Happen?

2. Reread pages 306–309. How do the pictures help you know that Rosa María is not really **forgetting** and losing things? **Analyze**

3. What special foods or activities do you have at family gatherings. **Analyze**

4. Why do you think some people like to celebrate by having parties? **Evaluate**

5. How are "Bobo's Celebration," on pages 300–301, and *Mice and Beans* alike? What do both parties have in common? **Reading/Writing Across Texts**

ROSA MARIA'S RICE AND BEANS

When you cook, you often mix **liquids** and **solids**. These different states of matter can change as you cook them. They may change in different ways.

Heating some solids can make them turn brown. Other solids become soft when you heat them. Heating liquids can make them boil. If you boil liquid long enough, it can change its state. It becomes a **gas**.

In the following recipes you will mix solids and liquids to make Rosa María's rice and beans.

Rice

Safety Note
Have an adult help you with this recipe.

What You Need

2	tablespoons vegetable oil
⅓	cup minced onion
⅓	cup minced bell pepper
1½	cups long grain white rice
1	14½-ounce can chicken or vegetable broth
¼	cup tomato sauce stirred into 1½ cups of water

What To Do

1. Pour the oil into a large skillet. Oil is a liquid.

2. Add the onion, bell pepper, and rice. These are solids. Sauté (SAW-tay), or fry, these solids over medium heat until rice is lightly toasted, and the vegetables are soft.

3. Add the liquids (broth and tomato sauce water) to the solids. Bring to a boil.

4. Cover, and turn the heat to low.

5. Simmer for 20 to 25 minutes, or until the liquid has been soaked up. Do not stir while simmering or the rice will be mushy.

Beans

What You Need

1	16-ounce bag dried pinto beans
1	large onion, chopped
4	cloves garlic, minced
2	14 ½ -ounce cans chicken or vegetable broth
2	14 ½ -ounce soup cans of water
	salt and pepper, add to taste

What To Do

1. Follow the directions on the back of the bag for cleaning and soaking the beans.
2. Drain the water (a liquid).
3. Combine the solids (beans, onions, and garlic) with the liquids (broth and water) in a large pot. Bring to a boil.
4. Reduce heat to low and simmer for 2 ½ to 3 hours. Stir often until beans are plump and soft.

Solid, Liquid, or Gas?

The same material can be in three different states—solid, liquid, and gas.

1. A solid has a definite size and shape. Ice is a solid. When water freezes, it becomes ice.

2. Liquid takes up space, but it does not have shape. Liquid in a container takes that container's shape. Water is a liquid.

3. Gas does not take up space or have shape. Steam is a gas. When water boils, it turns to steam.

FCAT Connect and Compare

1. What should you do to the beans while they are simmering? **Written Directions**

2. Think about the recipes and *Mice and Beans*. Rosa María planned a menu for the party. Write a menu that includes the food you would like to have at a party. **Reading/Writing Across Texts**

Science Activity

Think about your favorite recipe. Write about the solids, liquid, and gases in the recipe.

 Find out more about different states of matter at **www.macmillanmh.com**

ADVERTISE AN EVENT

Vary Words
Good writers strengthen and vary words to make their writing clear, interesting, and more exact.

> I use "annual" to tell how often field day happens.

> I vary my words when I give details.

Community Field Day!

The annual Washington Elementary School Field Day will take place on June 18.

Please join us for a day filled with exciting activities and terrific food. The fun starts at 1 p.m. at the school's football field.

This event is open to all students and their families. Come take part in sack races, a water balloon toss, and an obstacle course! A picnic will follow the games.

Contact Ms. Cahill for more information.

Writing Prompt

A flyer or a poster can advertise or tell about an event.

Think about an event.

Write an advertisement about this event.

FCAT Writer's Checklist

✓ **Focus:** My writing clearly advertises an event.

✓ **Organization:** I give information about what will happen at the event and where it will take place.

☑ **Support:** I strengthen and vary words to make my writing interesting and clear.

✓ **Conventions:** I capitalize and punctuate my sentences in the right places

Creating Stories

Talk About It

Do you like using words or pictures to tell your stories? Explain.

LOG ON Find out more about creating stories at **www.macmillanmh.com**

341

Making Stories Happen

Vocabulary

creating

familiar

occasions

memories

imagination

glamorous

FCAT Word Parts

Word **roots** and word parts can sometimes tell you the meaning of a new or unfamiliar word.

The word *imagination* comes from the Latin root *imag*. *Imag* means "likeness or picture."

Illustrator Joe Cepeda

When you read a book, do you think that the illustrator and author worked together? Sometimes that happens. But **creating** books isn't always like that. In fact, the process of making a book might surprise you. Often the author and illustrator never even talk to each other!

When writing a story, the author may give ideas about pictures to the illustrator. But sometimes the story is about something **familiar** to the illustrator, something that he or she has experienced in the past.

Author Pam Muñoz Ryan

For example, *Mice and Beans* is about a party. Joe Cepeda remembered **occasions** when his family had parties. They were to celebrate special events. He used his **memories**, his thoughts of those past events, to draw the pictures. Illustrators also use their **imagination**. They picture in their minds how characters and settings might look.

Being an author or illustrator may seem **glamorous**. It looks so interesting and exciting, but both jobs take a lot of hard work!

Reread for **Comprehension**

Text Structure
FCAT Main Idea and Details

Reading an article and using what you know from real life can help you make decisions, or **draw conclusions**, about the article's topic. Use the chart as you reread to draw conclusions about authors and illustrators.

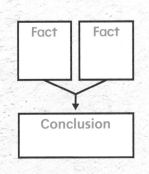

Comprehension

Genre

An **Autobiography** is a retelling of someone's life told by that person.

Text Structure

FCAT **Main Idea and Details**

As you read, use the **Conclusion** Chart.

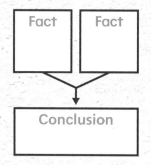

Read to Find Out
How does the author use her own life to write stories?

I moved into this house when I was four years old.

Me!

I had a lot of great friends growing up.

Stirring Up Memories

by
Pam Muñoz Ryan

Here I am with my
favorite doll!

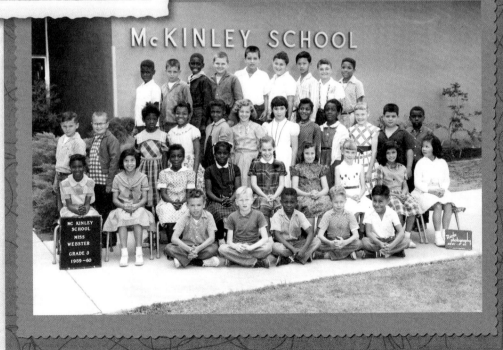

My third-grade class was very big. I'm sitting
in the middle and wearing a plaid dress.

Growing Up

I grew up in the San Joaquin (wah-keen) Valley in Bakersfield, California. This area is known for its hot, dry summers. It is often more than 100 degrees! When I was a young girl, I stayed cool by taking swimming lessons and eating ice pops. I also rode my bike to the library.

My friends and I liked to eat ice pops during the hot summers in California.

I loved the library for two important reasons. First, I could check out a pile of books and take them home with me. Second, the library was air-conditioned!

At my house, I was the oldest of three sisters. Next door to us, there lived another three girls. They were all younger than me, too. Whenever we played together, I was in charge of what we did. I was the director of the play, or the mom in a pretend family. Sometimes I was the doctor who saved their lives!

Here I am opening presents at my birthday party with my friends.

I was also the oldest of the 23 cousins in my family. When we had a family party at my grandmother's house, I was the boss again. I would say, "Let's pretend this is a circus or a school or a jungle . . . " Then I would tell everyone what they should do and say. I didn't know it at the time, but I was already **creating** stories!

I was about 17 years old at this family gathering. I'm second from the right in the back row, holding one of my baby cousins.

**This family party was at my uncle's house.
I'm sitting at the table wearing the black sweater.**

Some of my favorite **memories** are of those times at my grandmother's house. The kitchen always smelled like onions, garlic, and roasted peppers. There was often a big pot of beans on the stove. A pan of Spanish rice was cooking next to it.

When we were all together, it was crowded and noisy. Sound **familiar**? My story, *Mice and Beans*, is about a big family gathering and a grandmother who loves to cook!

FCAT Main Idea and Details
Why do you think Pam Muñoz Ryan's favorite memories are of her grandmother's house?

Finding an Idea

Readers always want to know where I get my ideas. I wish I could say that I go to an idea store and buy them. As far as I know, there is no such place.

I like to visit schools.
Children always ask me
where I get the ideas for
my books.

Mrs. Pam Muñoz Ryan

Real-life people like Eleanor Roosevelt (left) and Amelia Earhart (below) sometimes inspire me to write stories.

Sometimes my ideas come from something interesting I might have read about in a book. Sometimes they come from real life, like those times at my grandmother's house. Of course, the clever mice in *Mice and Beans* didn't come from real life. They came from my **imagination**.

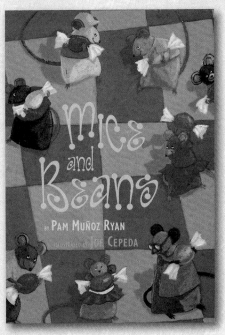

For *Mice and Beans,* I wanted to write a story about a grandmother getting ready for a big family party. I wondered what kind of party it could be.

I decided on a birthday party for the youngest grandchild. In my mind, I saw the grandmother preparing for a week. Each day, she would carefully clean her kitchen.

I thought of my grandmother, Esperanza, when I wrote *Mice and Beans.* In the photo above she is holding me when I was a baby.

Below is a picture of one of my own family parties. It is my son Tyler's birthday.

I wondered why my character was so tidy. Was she worried about ants? Or maybe mice? As I kept thinking, I imagined what it would be like if she already had mice but didn't know it. That idea made the story seem funnier to me. Then, one thing led to another.

That's what happens when I'm writing. I start out with one idea. Then, the more I think about it, the more choices I have for the story. Sometimes I try out different ideas on paper. Then I choose the one I like best.

Now that I'm an adult, it's my turn to cook special foods for my friends and family to enjoy.

My Favorite Recipe

Salsa

2 large	tomatoes; seeded and chopped
1 to 2	chile peppers; seeded & chopped
1/3 c	chopped green onions
2 tb	chopped fresh cilantro
2 tb	lime juice
1/4 ts	salt

Combine all ingredients. Mix well and then cover. Refrigerate until serving time.

Once I've thought of an idea, it's time to start writing.

Many people think that writers look far away to find their stories. The truth is that most writers look within. They stir up memories and then sprinkle them with their imagination.

FCAT Main Idea and Details
Why do you think Pam Muñoz Ryan says that most writers look inside themselves for story ideas? Explain.

A Writer's Life

Readers often think that a writer's life is **glamorous** with fancy cars and clothes. For a very few, that might be true, but my life is much different than that.

I work at my home in California, near San Diego. I don't have to dress up to go to work. I don't take long train rides because my desk is in my house. I get up early, eat breakfast, and go straight to my office to write.

Working at home means I can walk from my breakfast table right to my office.

Sammie and Buddy keep me company when I want to work and when I want to play.

I have two friends who love to watch me work. They are my dogs, Buddy and Sammie. Almost every day, I take them for a walk, either in my neighborhood or on the beach.

For part of the year, the house is mostly quiet. My husband, Jim, and I have four children, two girls and twin boys. The girls are grown up now, but the boys are still in college. They come home during the summer. Since we live near the Pacific Ocean, there is a lot of going back and forth to the beach.

My husband, Jim, and I enjoy taking Buddy and Sammie to the beach.

Many of my favorite memories are of times spent at home.

My childhood home

Today when my children are all together in our house for family **occasions**, it is crowded and noisy. It's just like when I was a little girl. Sometimes I even cook rice and beans! During these times, we're creating new memories. Maybe someday they'll give me the idea for another story!

Stirring Up Ideas with Pam Muñoz Ryan

Pam Muñoz Ryan likes to visit classrooms. Children often ask her how to become a writer. "If you want to be a writer, first become a reader," Pam says. "Daydream every day and pretend often. That's where ideas live—in your imagination. If you think of a story, write it down and save it. Someday, it might be the seed that grows into something magnificent."

Other books written by Pam Muñoz Ryan

 Find out more about Pam Muñoz Ryan at **www.macmillanmh.com**

FCAT Author's Purpose

Pam explains what she did during the summer when she was a girl. What do you like to do in the summer? Write a paragraph about your summers.

FCAT Comprehension Check

Retell the Story

Use the Retelling Cards to retell the selection.

Retelling Cards

Think and Compare

1. Why is this selection titled *Stirring Up Memories*? Use details and information from the article to support your answer. **Text Structure: Main Idea and Details**

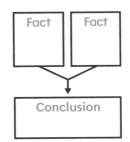

2. Reread page 348. What did Pam enjoy doing as a child that she still loves to do? **Apply**

3. What might you like about being a writer? **Evaluate**

4. Why might some people think that being a writer is **glamorous**? **Synthesize**

5. Read "Making Stories Happen" on pages 342–343. How is Joe Cepeda's way of working like Pam's way? **Reading/Writing Across Texts**

BRUSH DANCE

by Robin Bernard

A dot,
    a blot,
        a smidge,
            a smear.
and just a little squiggle here...
A dab,
    a dash,
        a splish,
           a splat.
that's how Patrick paints a cat!

CRAYONS

by Marchette Chute

I've colored a picture with crayons.

I'm not very pleased with the sun.

I'd like it much stronger and brighter.

And more like the actual one.

I've tried with a crayon that's yellow.

I've tried with a crayon that's red.

But none of it looks like the sunlight

I carry around in my head.

FCAT Connect and Compare

1. Which words from the poem "Brush Dance" use onomatopoeia? **Onomatopoeia**

2. Think about the speaker from the poem "Crayons" and Pam Muñoz Ryan from *Stirring Up Memories*. How are they alike? **Reading/Writing Across Texts**

LOG ON Find out more about poetry at **www.macmillanmh.com**

Write a Poem

FCAT Writer's Craft

Vary Words
Good writers use
precise words to
show their emotions
and voice.

Precise words can
show voice.

I use precise
words to show
emotion.

Tea Party
by Brittany H.

A rainy Sunday, what should we do?
Mom said, "I've got an idea for you.
We'll make fancy snacks and iced tea.
I'll serve you, and you serve me!"
What a wonderful thing to do,
On a gloomy Sunday for just us two.

Writing Prompt

A poem usually includes rhythm.

Think about what you would like to write a poem about.

Now, write a poem.

FCAT Writer's Checklist

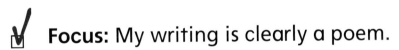

☑ **Focus:** My writing is clearly a poem.

☑ **Organization:** My poem includes a main idea and details.

☑ **Support:** I use precise words to show emotion and voice.

☑ **Conventions:** My punctuation is correct. My poem has rhythm.

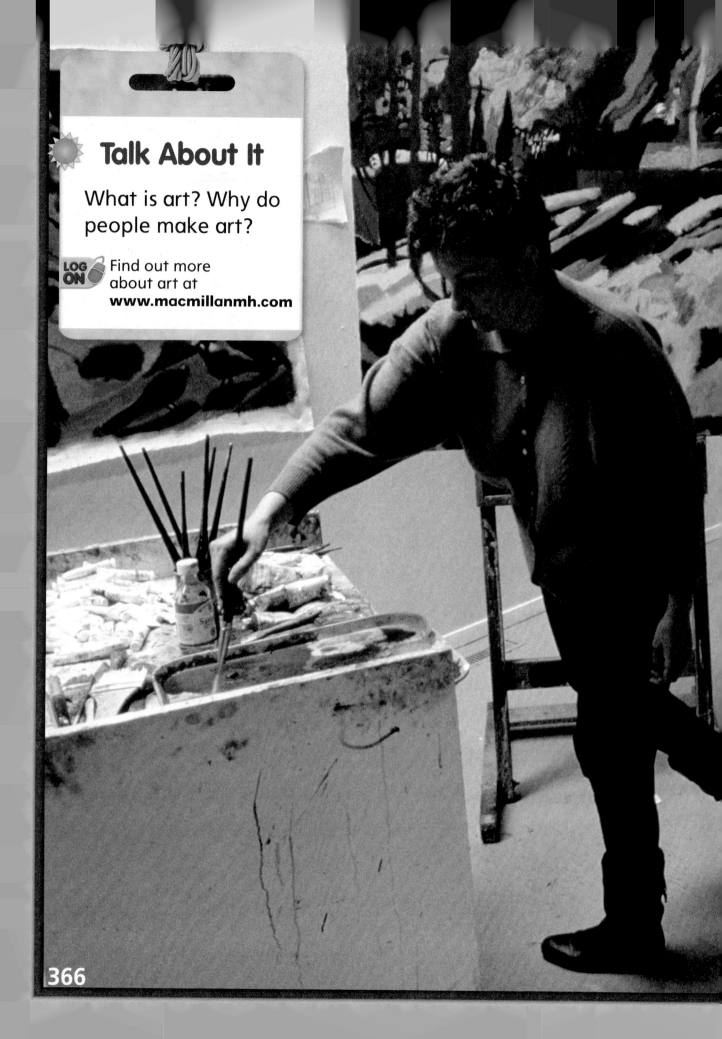

Talk About It

What is art? Why do people make art?

LOG ON Find out more about art at **www.macmillanmh.com**

366

WORLDS OF ART

Vocabulary

impossible

treasures

watch

talent

pleasant

A Chinese artist creates a bear out of ice.

People enjoy the ice slide at the Winter Carnival in Quebec, Canada.

Snow sculptures in Canada

Frozen Art

Does it seem **impossible** for a block of ice to become a work of art? Some artists make it happen. Using special tools, the sculptors make interesting figures and shapes out of ice.

Ice art is popular in many places around the world. In Harbin, China, nearly a million people attend the Ice Lantern Festival to see the ice sculptures. In Canada, people go to the Winter Carnival in Quebec. Here they can stay at a hotel made entirely of ice!

So the next time it snows, imagine what beautiful artistic **treasures** you could create. Practice hard and **watch** your sculpture come to life. You'll see a wonderful, one-of-a kind piece of art!

LOG ON Find out more about ice art at **www.macmillanmh.com**

Elephant Artists

Think only people can paint pictures? Think again!

In Thailand, two elephants named Boon Yang and Bird are artists. With paintbrushes clutched in their trunks, they create works of art. You might not think elephants have much **talent**, but these two are very capable artists. Their paintings sell for more than a thousand dollars each!

Boon Yang and Bird used to work with people clearing trees in forests. But the time came when their help was no longer needed. Two human artists wanted to find a **pleasant** way to keep the elephants busy. Now Boon Yang and Bird spend their time painting, which they seem to enjoy. Some of their paintings even hang in museums!

◀ Trainers encourage elephant artists Boon Yang and Bird to paint.

▲ This is one of the elephants' paintings.

369

This exhibit shows what people from the Stone Age might have looked like.

Comprehension

Genre

A **Nonfiction Article** gives information about real people, places, and events.

Text Structure

FCAT Author's Purpose

When you read, you should identify an author's purpose in the text.

Music of the Stone Age

How do we know that people made music thousands of years ago?

Today, recorded music surrounds us. You can buy CDs of your favorite music. You can hear singers on the radio. You can even **watch** them on TV. Thousands of years from now, people will know about our music because we have made recordings of it.

Thousands of years ago, recording music was **impossible**. So how do we know that people long ago played music? Because scientists have found flutes that are 9,000 years old! The flutes were found in China, in the Yellow River Valley. Here, scientists unearthed all sorts of **treasures**, including 36 flutes.

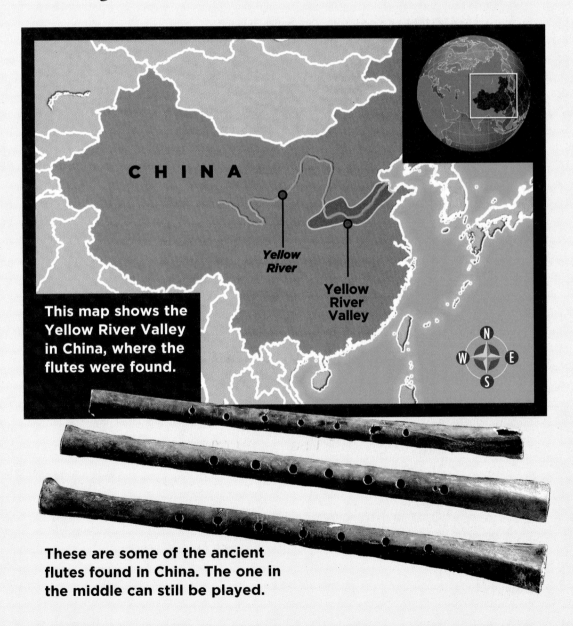

CHINA

Yellow River

Yellow River Valley

This map shows the Yellow River Valley in China, where the flutes were found.

These are some of the ancient flutes found in China. The one in the middle can still be played.

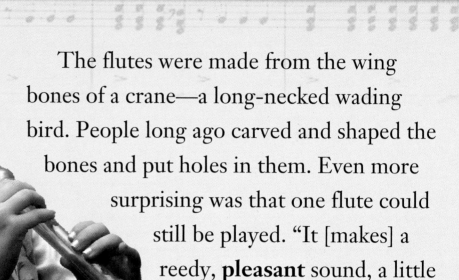

The flutes were made from the wing bones of a crane—a long-necked wading bird. People long ago carved and shaped the bones and put holes in them. Even more surprising was that one flute could still be played. "It [makes] a reedy, **pleasant** sound, a little thin, like a recorder," one scientist described.

The ancient flutes made a sound like a modern recorder.

What Is Sound?

Sound is a kind of energy that you can hear. Sound is made when something vibrates, or moves quickly back and forth. When something vibrates, it makes the air vibrate, too. Vibrating air carries the sound you hear.

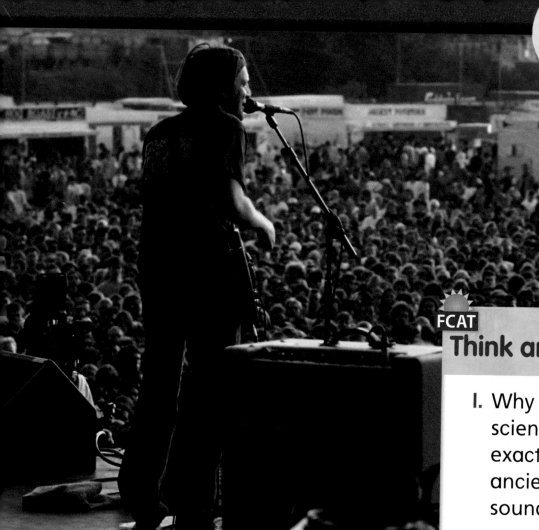

Today, people can enjoy recorded music as well as live music at concerts like this one.

No one knows for sure what type of music the people from the Stone Age played. Did it sound like the music of today? Did people have musical **talent** and perform concerts? Did people sing along? We can only wonder what their music might have sounded like!

FCAT
Think and Compare

1. Why don't scientists know exactly what ancient music sounded like?

2. How do you think music from the Stone Age was different from today's music?

3. What instruments are used to make your favorite kind of music?

4. Why did the author write this selection?

373

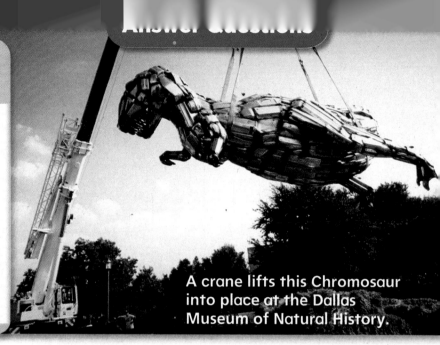

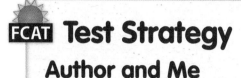

FCAT Test Strategy

Author and Me
The answer is not on the page. Think about everything you have read to figure out the best answer.

A crane lifts this Chromosaur into place at the Dallas Museum of Natural History.

The Art of Recycling

An artist in Mexico makes tiny furniture from bottle caps. Another artist in Liberia cuts up old flip-flop sandals to create a toy helicopter. For hundreds of years, people around the world have made artwork and toys from trash. They still do. In some places, trash may be the only material that artists and toymakers can afford.

Artists in the United States recycle, too. John Kearney is a 74-year-old grandfather from Chicago, Illinois. He is also an artist who thinks junk is great for making art. He once made three giant dinosaur sculptures out of chrome car bumpers. He called them Chromosaurs. One of them was 18 feet tall!

Recycling can be a lot more than just tossing trash into a bin. A work of art can be beautiful whether it's made with paint, clay, or even recycled trash.

This toy helicopter is made from old flip-flop sandals.

Go on ▶

FCAT **Now answer Numbers I through 4. Base your answers on the article "The Art of Recycling."**

1 What is the main idea of this story?
- Ⓐ There are many artists in Mexico.
- Ⓑ Art is always made from trash.
- Ⓒ Artists can use trash to make art and toys.
- Ⓓ Car bumpers make good toys.

2 What do the Chromosaurs and the helicopter have in common?
- Ⓐ They are made from car parts.
- Ⓑ They are made from thrown-away materials.
- Ⓒ They are tiny copies of big things.
- Ⓓ They are children's toys.

3 How did Chromosaurs get their name?
- Ⓐ from the scientist who found them
- Ⓑ from their big teeth
- Ⓒ because they are made of chrome
- Ⓓ because it sounded good

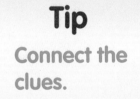

Tip
Connect the clues.

4 How does John Kearney recycle? Use details and information from the article to support your answer.

READ
THINK
EXPLAIN

Write to a Prompt

Maria wrote a story with a beginning, a middle, and an end about a parrot that was an artist.

I wrote the events in the order they happened.

The Painting Parrot

Grandpa and I went to the zoo to see a parrot that was supposed to be able to paint. I watched the bird smear green globs of paint on some paper. "Anybody could do that," I said to Grandpa. "Let's go see the gorillas." Suddenly the parrot started painting really fast. It squawked, and I thought it sounded like "Look!" So I looked. The parrot had the paper in its beak. On it was a picture of a green gorilla. I guess that parrot can paint! And it can talk, too!

Your Writing Prompt

Now it's your turn to write a short story about what might happen next.

FCAT In a story, something always happens after the beginning event.

Think about a time when you were surprised by what happened next.

Write a short story telling what happened.

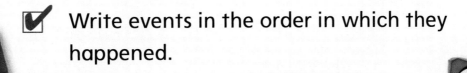

Writing Hints for Prompts

☑ Ask yourself, who will read my story?

☑ Plan your writing before beginning.

☑ Write events in the order in which they happened.

☑ Use your best spelling, grammar, and punctuation.

INVENTIONS
Then and Now

Talk About It

Describe some of the inventions that make your life easier. Do you know who created them?

LOG ON Find out more about inventions at **www.macmillanmh.com**

379

Kid Inventors Then and Now

by Kali Capria

Chester Greenwood was a fifteen-year-old who lived in the 1800s. Chester's parents **allowed** him to play outside. They let him go out even in the wintertime. Chester lived in Maine, where the winters are cold. There is lots of snow and **powerful**, strong winds. Chester would get very cold, but he wouldn't wear a hat.

Chester decided to create something to solve his problem. He **invented** a way to keep his ears warm. He used an **instrument**, or tool, to bend wire into loops.

Greenwood's Ear Protectors

Worn by Millions

25c

"Blizzard Proof"

This is an ad for Chester Greenwood's earmuffs.

380

His grandmother then sewed fur onto them. Chester had created the first pair of earmuffs!

More than 100 years later, cold, snowy weather also gave ten-year-old K-K Gregory an idea. Snow kept getting up her coat sleeves. She looked in many stores to find an item to solve her problem. She couldn't find any good **products**. So K-K made a **design** for a new kind of glove. She drew and described something she called *wristies*. Wristies are long gloves without fingers. They were a big hit with people living in cold places all over the world!

K-K Gregory tries out her invention.

Reread for Comprehension

Reread

FCAT Compare and Contrast

Rereading can help you **compare and contrast** information in an article. To compare means to tell how things are alike. To contrast means to tell how they are different. Reread the selection and use the chart to compare and contrast these inventors.

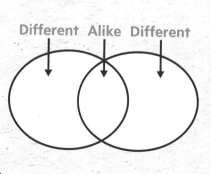

Different Alike Different

Genre
A **Biography** is the story of a person's life written by another person.

Reread
 FCAT **Compare and Contrast**
As you read, use the **Compare and Contrast** Chart.

Different   Alike   Different

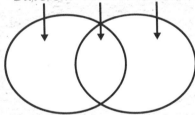

Read to Find Out
How are these inventors alike? How are they different?

African-American
INVENTORS

by Jim Haskins
illustrated by Eric Velasquez

Award
Winning
Illustrator

STATES PATENT OFFICE

H E GOODE OF CHICAGO ILLINOIS

CABINET-BED

Introduction

Inventors create new things. Their inventions solve problems or make life better in some way. Throughout our history, African Americans have **invented** many important things.

◄ John Lee Love received a patent for a pencil sharpener in 1887.

Garrett Morgan received a patent for an early type of traffic signal on November 20, 1923. ►

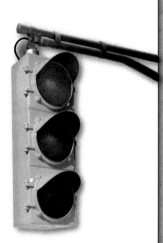

◄ John Purdy and James Sadgwar patented a folding chair in 1889.

Benjamin Banneker

Benjamin Banneker was born on a farm in Maryland in 1731. At that time, Maryland was one of thirteen British colonies in North America.

Most African-American people in the colonies were enslaved, but Benjamin's parents were free. Because Benjamin was born to a free family, he could go to school.

▲ Benjamin Banneker grew up near Baltimore, Maryland, in the mid-1700s.

In the 1700s many schoolhouses were one room. ▼

Benjamin went to a local school for boys. He was so good at math that he soon knew more than his teacher. After he finished his education, Benjamin worked on the family farm.

Benjamin's life changed when he was twenty years old. He met a man who owned a pocket watch. The watch had been made in Europe. Benjamin was so interested in the watch that the man let him keep it.

Benjamin studied the watch, its parts, and the way it was made. He decided to make his own clock out of wood. It was the first clock ever made in North America.

◄ Benjamin Banneker's wooden clock worked perfectly for more than 40 years.

Benjamin used his clock to measure the movements of the stars. He used math to figure out the position of the stars, sun, moon, and planets. Years later, he wrote an almanac. An almanac is a book that lists the positions of the sun, moon, and planets for every day of the year.

Benjamin Bannaker's
PENNSYLVANIA, DELAWARE, MARY-
LAND, AND VIRGINIA
ALMANAC,
FOR THE
YEAR of our LORD 1795;
Being the Third after Leap-Year.

PHILADELPHIA:
Printed for WILLIAM GIBBONS, Cherry Street

▲ Benjamin published almanacs from 1792 to 1797.

Benjamin wrote a new almanac every year for six years. People read it to find out when the sun and moon would rise and set. They read it to find out how the weather would change each season. Many farmers used Benjamin's almanacs so they would know when to plant their crops. He was as famous for his almanacs as he was for his clock.

▲ Farming in the 1700s was done by hand. Tractors and other farm machines had not been invented yet.

Sarah E. Goode

We know quite a bit about Benjamin Banneker. We know very little about Sarah E. Goode. What we do know is that she was the first African-American woman to receive a patent for an invention.

A patent is a legal paper. It is given out by the United States government in Washington, D.C. A person who invents something can get a patent to prove that he or she was the first to have made it. No one else can say they invented that same thing.

Sarah Goode received her patent in 1885. ▼

UNITED STATES PATENT OFFICE.

SARAH E. GOODE, OF CHICAGO, ILLINOIS.

CABINET-BED.

SPECIFICATION forming part of Letters Patent No. 322,177, dated July 14, 188

Application filed November 12, 1883. (No model.)

To all whom it may concern:

Be it known that I, SARAH E. GOODE, a citizen of the United States, residing at Chicago, in the county of Cook and State of Illinois, have invented a certain new and useful Improvement in Cabinet-Beds, of which the following is a full, clear, concise, and exact description, reference being had to the accompanying drawings, forming a part of this specification.

This invention relate tional bedsteads adapte when not in use, so as and made generally to of furniture when so fo The objects of this

ding. The folding sections B C the stationary section A on o thereof, so that when unfolded section A becomes the middle bed, while the folding sectio respective end portions the the stationary section A in the length of the bed this well-known construc may be obtained

Sarah Goode owned a furniture ▶ store in the 1880s.

▲ In the 1880s and 1890s many people moved to Chicago to find jobs.

Sarah was born in a southern state in 1850. She was born into slavery. When slavery ended, Sarah was a teenager. She was able to go to school once she was free. After she received her education, Sarah moved to Chicago, Illinois.

Sarah must have been smart and hard working. By the time she was 35 years old, she owned her own business. Sarah Goode was the owner of a furniture store.

Many African-American people were moving from southern states to northern states in the 1870s and 1880s. They moved into apartment houses. Sometimes many people slept in one room. This was because many people did not have enough money to rent their own rooms.

Sarah had the idea of making a bed that could fit in a small space. It could fold up during the day and unfold at night. She worked out a **design**. Then she made a model.

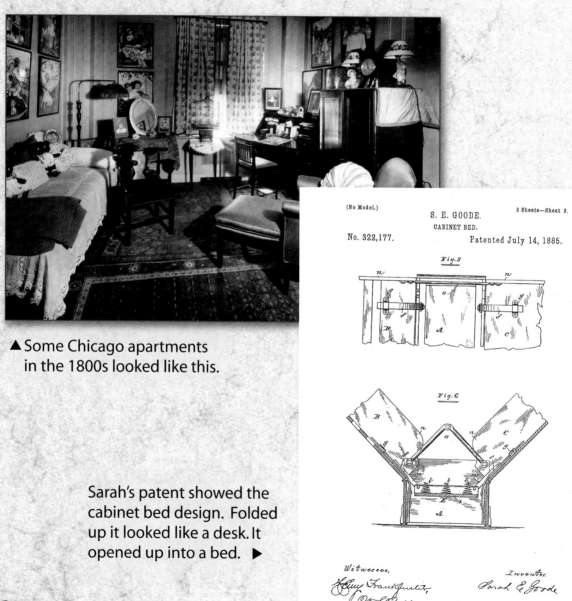

▲ Some Chicago apartments in the 1800s looked like this.

Sarah's patent showed the cabinet bed design. Folded up it looked like a desk. It opened up into a bed. ▶

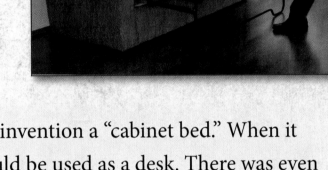

Different folding bed designs have been made over the years.

Sarah called her invention a "cabinet bed." When it was folded up, it could be used as a desk. There was even a place for keeping pens and paper.

Sarah did not want anyone else to copy her invention. She made sure of that by getting a patent.

We do not know how many cabinet beds Sarah made. We do know that her idea is still helpful for people. Folding beds are still in use today.

FCAT Compare and Contrast

In what ways did Benjamin Banneker's and Sarah Goode's inventions help people?

George Washington Carver

George Washington Carver was born in Missouri about 1861. Like Sarah E. Goode, he was born into slavery. His family was enslaved by a couple named Carver. George was raised by Mr. and Mrs. Carver.

George loved the Carver farm, with all of its plants and animals. He planted his own garden. Soon, he knew so much about plants that people called him the Plant Doctor.

▲ This is a painting of a typical farm in the 1870s.

▲ George Washington Carver at school.

▲ George graduated from college in 1894.

George wanted to go to school to learn more about plants. Slavery was over, so he was free to leave the Carver farm. It took him twenty years to get enough education and save enough money to enter college.

George went to college in Iowa. He was the first African-American student at the school. He studied farming and learned even more about plants. When he graduated, he became a teacher.

▲ George taught at his college in Alabama.

George taught at Tuskegee Institute in Alabama. It was a college for African-American people. He studied plants at the college. George told farmers that peanuts and sweet potatoes were good crops to grow. He found that he could make 118 different **products** from the sweet potato. These included soap, coffee, and glue.

▲ George told farmers which vegetables were useful crops to grow.

George learned that he could do even more with peanuts. He made over 300 different products from peanuts. Some of these were peanut butter, ice cream, paper, ink, shaving cream, and shampoo. George only received three patents for the products he invented. He believed that most of them should belong to everyone.

▲ George spent many hours working in his laboratory.

Patricia Bath, M.D.

Patricia Bath was born more than 75 years after George Washington Carver. Patricia was born in a northern state. She grew up in the New York City neighborhood of Harlem.

Like George Washington Carver, she was still young when she began to study living things. Her special interest was human diseases. After high school, she got a job helping people who studied cancer.

▲ Patricia Bath grew up in Harlem, New York, in the 1940s.

In college, Patricia studied chemistry. Then she went to medical school. She decided to study eye diseases. She wanted to find out how to remove cataracts.

Cataracts are like clouds on the lens of the eye. They make everything look cloudy. Patricia designed an **instrument** for removing cataracts. It gives off a **powerful** beam of light that breaks up the cataract. Then it can be removed.

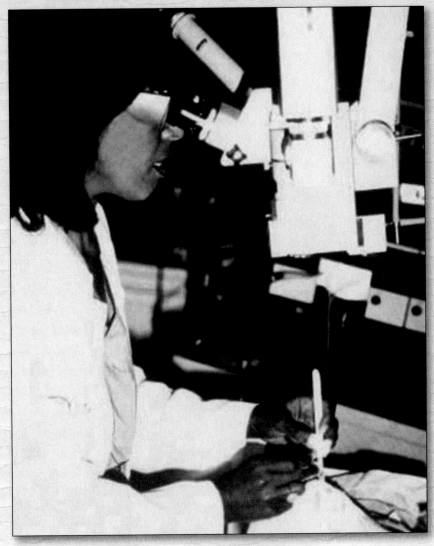

▲ Dr. Patricia Bath performing eye surgery.

In 1988 Patricia received a patent for the instrument she invented. She was the first African-American woman to get a patent for a medical invention. Since then she has invented other eye instruments. Her work has **allowed** many people to see again.

FCAT **Compare and Contrast**
What do Patricia Bath and George Washington Carver have in common? How are their lives different?

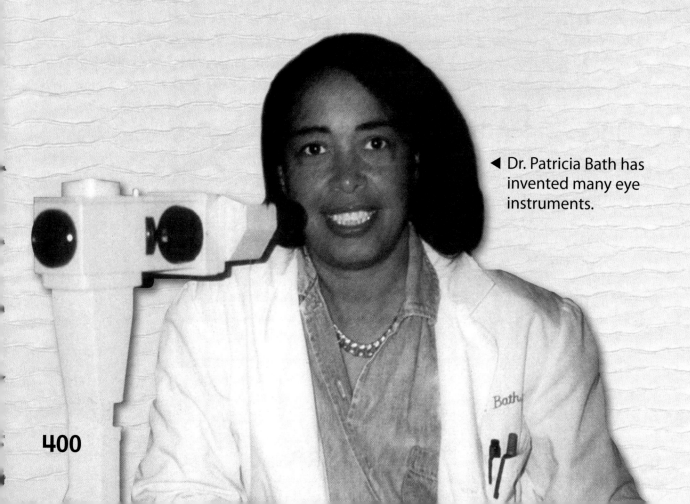

◄ Dr. Patricia Bath has invented many eye instruments.

Inventors Change the World

The stories of these four inventors show how African-American inventors have helped make life better for all Americans throughout history. Benjamin Banneker helped people keep time and know the positions of the stars and planets. Sarah Goode made furniture for people to use in small homes. George Washington Carver made hundreds of products from sweet potatoes and peanuts. Dr. Patricia Bath invented a cure for one kind of blindness. The world is better because of their work.

Meet the Author

Jim Haskins has written more than 100 books. Many of his books are about African Americans and great things they have done. Some are about the history and culture of Africa.

Jim has always loved to read and learn about famous people. He says, "I did not have any favorite childhood authors, but mostly enjoyed reading the *Encyclopaedia Britannica* and *World Book*, Volumes A through Z."

Other books written by Jim Haskins

LOG ON Find out more about Jim Haskins at
www.macmillanmh.com

FCAT Author's Purpose

Jim Haskins wants readers to learn about certain inventors. Write a paragraph about the person you think is most interesting. Be sure to give reasons for why you think the way you do.

FCAT Comprehension Check

Retell the Story

Use the Retelling Cards to retell the selection.

Retelling Cards

Think and Compare

READ
THINK
EXPLAIN

1. How are all the inventors in this article alike and different? Use details and information from the selection to support your answer.
Reread: Compare and Contrast

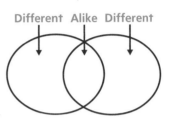

Different Alike Different

2. Reread pages 392–393. Why do you think Sarah Goode's cabinet bed was so popular? **Analyze**

3. Which inventions in this selection do you think helped the most people? **Evaluate**

4. Why do you think most inventors want patents for their inventions? **Synthesize**

5. How do the **products** in *African-American Inventors* compare to those in "Kid Inventors Then and Now" on pages 380–381?
Reading/Writing Across Texts

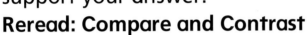

Science

Inventors Time Line

1731 - Benjamin Banneker is born.

1700	1750	1800

1792 - Benjamin Banneker publishes an almanac. It helps **predict** weather for the coming year.

A time line is helpful for finding out when important **events** took place. The time line on these pages gives you **information** about some of the inventors you've read about this week. You can see when they were born and when they created their inventions.

404

1858 - Chester Greenwood is born.

1942 - Patricia Bath is born.

1988 - Dr. Bath receives a patent.

1850   **1900**   **1950**   **2000**

1873 - Chester Greenwood invents earmuffs.

1983 - K-K Gregory is born.

1993 - K-K Gregory invents Wristies.

 Connect and Compare

1. Which was invented first, earmuffs or Wristies? How do you know? **Time Line**

2. Think about this time line and *African-American Inventors*. Choose one inventor from the selection and make a time line of his or her life. **Reading/Writing Across Texts**

 Science Activity

Research another famous inventor. Make a time line that shows important events in his or her life.

LOG ON Find out more about inventors at **www.macmillanmh.com**

405

Writer's Craft

Important Details
Good writers include
important details in
their writing to help
make it clear as well
as interesting.

This important detail
tells about Grandpa
Ben.

This details is
important, too.

Grandpa Ben

by Michael O.

My grandfather, Ben Rogers, is
an interesting man. He was born in
1948 in California, and he has lived
in ten different states. He married
Grandma Lena when he was 24.
They have four children.

Grandpa Ben is a scientist and
an inventor. He works carefully
in his lab. I always know when
Grandpa Ben has a new idea.
His eyes open wide, and he speaks
very quickly. Many people call him
Dr. Rogers, but he is Grandpa Ben
to me!

Writing Prompt

Most people have interesting information to share about their lives.

Think about someone you know well.

Write what you know about this person.

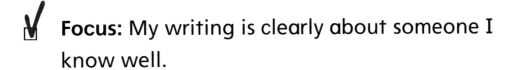

FCAT Writer's Checklist

✓ **Focus:** My writing is clearly about someone I know well.

✓ **Organization:** My writing sticks to the topic.

✓ **Support:** I include important details about the person I am writing about.

✓ **Conventions:** My sentences begin in different ways. My writing flows when it is read aloud.

OTHER PEOPLE, OTHER PLACES

Talk About It

What can you tell about this land? What clues does the picture give you about the person?

LOG ON Find out more about other people and other places at **www.macmillanmh.com**

E-mails from Other Places

e-mail

Write   Send   Reply   Print   Delete   @ Addresses

From: gram@example.com
To: aki@example.com

Dear Aki,

It was so nice to visit you in Michigan, but I'm glad to be back home in Japan. I showed Grandfather pictures from your soccer game. "Look at her shin guards and gloves!" he **exclaimed**. He sounded very surprised. I explained that you are a **goalie**. It's your job to guard the goal and keep the other team from scoring. Grandfather's **concern** is for your safety. He is worried that you might get hurt. Now he knows that what you wear helps keep you safe.

Love,
Grandmother

410

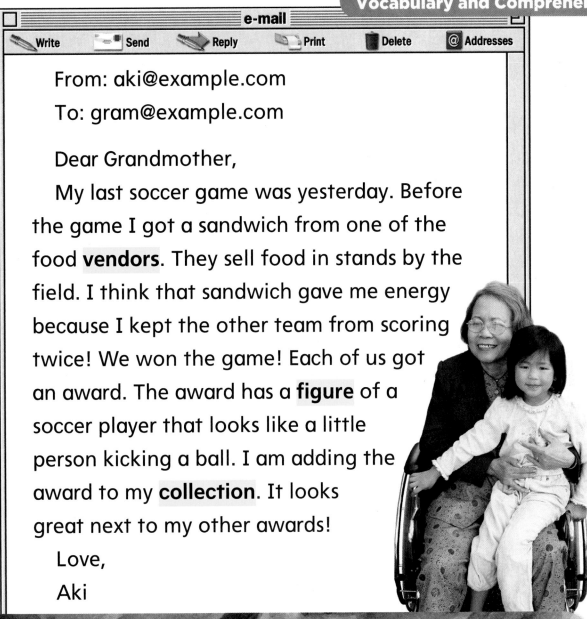

e-mail

Write | Send | Reply | Print | Delete | @ Addresses

From: aki@example.com
To: gram@example.com

Dear Grandmother,

My last soccer game was yesterday. Before the game I got a sandwich from one of the food **vendors**. They sell food in stands by the field. I think that sandwich gave me energy because I kept the other team from scoring twice! We won the game! Each of us got an award. The award has a **figure** of a soccer player that looks like a little person kicking a ball. I am adding the award to my **collection**. It looks great next to my other awards!

Love,
Aki

Reread for **Comprehension**

Reread
FCAT Plot

Rereading a selection can help you better understand the plot, including the **characters** and the **setting**. Reread the e-mails and use the chart to help you understand the people in the e-mails and where they take place.

Characters	Setting

Genre

Realistic Fiction is a made-up story that could happen in real life.

Reread

Plot

As you read, use your Characters and Setting Chart.

Characters	Setting

Read to Find Out

Who are Babu and Bernardi? Why do they get along so well?

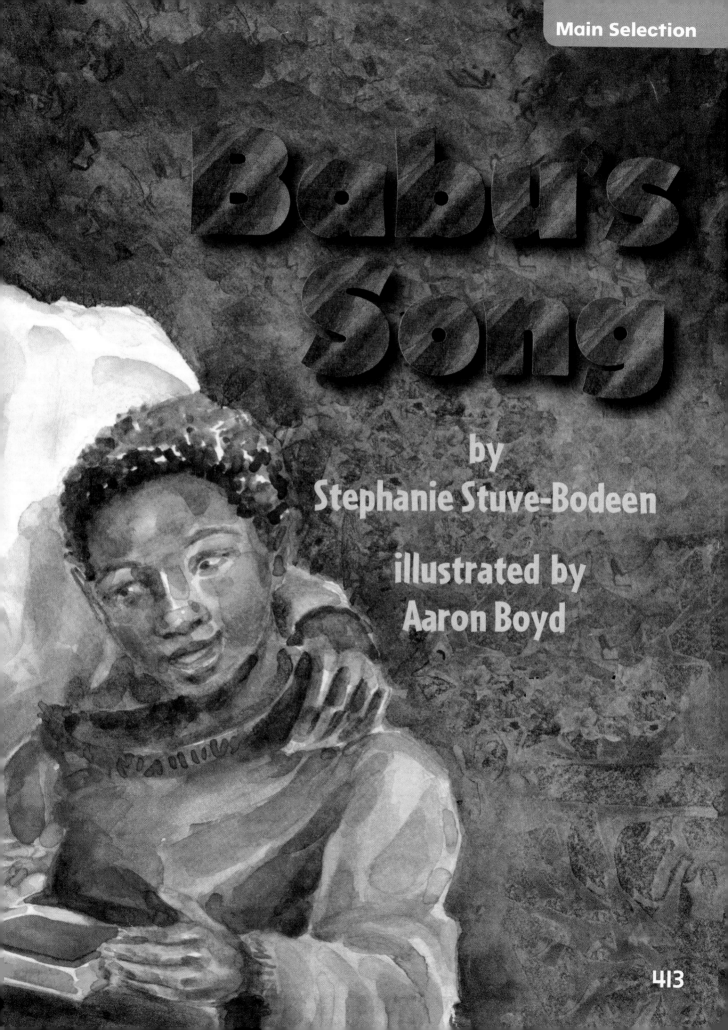

Babu's Song

by
Stephanie Stuve-Bodeen

illustrated by
Aaron Boyd

413

Bernardi ran hard, kicking the ball toward the goal. His arms pumping and his heart racing, he didn't care that he was the only boy on the field not wearing a school uniform.

He loved soccer and his one **concern** was making a goal. With a final kick so powerful that it knocked him on his back, Bernardi sent the ball flying past the **goalie** and into the net.

Bernardi lay on the grassy field, catching his breath. A boy helped him up, then ran after the others going into the school. Bernardi wished he could go to school like the other children. He liked to learn, and thought he could be a good student. Besides, then he could play soccer every day, not just when the schoolboys needed an extra player. Bernardi lived with his grandfather, Babu, and they did not have enough money for school.

Slowly Bernardi walked home.

When Bernardi walked in, Babu gave him a hug. This was how he said hello, because an illness had taken his voice a long time ago.

"Hello, Babu," Bernardi said. "I made a goal today." Bernardi loved telling Babu his soccer stories.

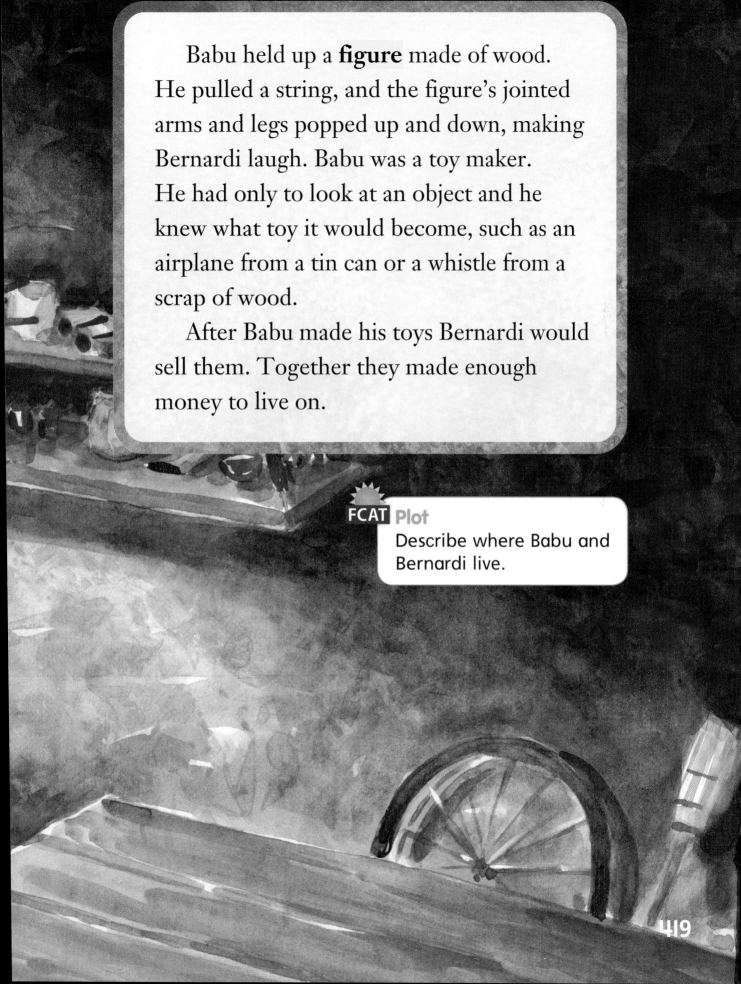

Babu held up a **figure** made of wood.
He pulled a string, and the figure's jointed
arms and legs popped up and down, making
Bernardi laugh. Babu was a toy maker.
He had only to look at an object and he
knew what toy it would become, such as an
airplane from a tin can or a whistle from a
scrap of wood.

After Babu made his toys Bernardi would
sell them. Together they made enough
money to live on.

FCAT Plot

Describe where Babu and
Bernardi live.

Babu made tea for Bernardi and himself. After they finished Bernardi took an old bag from beside the door, waved good-bye to Babu, and set off for the market. As he walked, Bernardi hummed a tune. It was a song that Babu had sung when he had his voice. Humming it made Bernardi wish Babu could still speak.

"Anything for Babu?" Bernardi asked the **vendors** when he reached the market.

The vendors gave Bernardi bits of string or paper, anything that Babu might be able to use to make his toys. Mama Valentina, who sold salt, called to Bernardi. She handed him a plastic gunnysack. Bernardi thanked her as he stuffed it into his bag, even though he didn't think Babu could use it.

As Bernardi walked home, he passed a shop downtown and stopped to look in the window. There among the bright bolts of cloth and shiny pots was a new soccer ball. It was just what he had always wanted. Bernardi pressed his face against the window and looked at the price. It was more than it cost to go to school!

Slowly Bernardi backed away from the window. He did not hum as he walked home.

That evening Babu and Bernardi ate beans and rice by the light of the kerosene lamp. Babu put something by Bernardi's plate. Bernardi picked it up and held it closer to the light. It looked like a tin of lard. He opened the lid and heard a small tinkling.

"A music box!" Bernardi **exclaimed**, and listened again. It was rough and tinny, but he recognized the tune. It was Babu's song.

Bernardi hugged Babu, and together they listened to the music. That night, for the first time in many nights, Bernardi fell asleep listening to Babu's song.

The next Saturday was a busy one for Bernardi, as it was the day he sold toys to tourists. He set up shop on his favorite corner downtown, arranging the toys on the curb.

Bernardi cranked the music box and listened to Babu's song tinkle out. He had sold a few things when a woman picked up the music box. She asked how much it was, but Bernardi said it wasn't for sale.

The woman did not give up. She told Bernardi that she wanted the music box for her **collection**, but still Bernardi shook his head. The woman held out a handful of money. Bernardi's eyes widened. It would be more than enough to buy the ball in the store window.

Bernardi picked up the music box. He thought about the brand-new ball and how it would feel when he kicked it. Surely Babu could make another music box.

Bernardi swallowed hard and took the money.

After Bernardi sold all the toys he did not go home. He took the money and headed for the shops down the street.

When Bernardi got home, Babu was cleaning. He looked up at Bernardi holding the empty bag.

"I sold everything, Babu!" Bernardi said, trying to sound cheerful, but then a tear rolled down his face. Babu went over to Bernardi. He wiped his grandson's face and waited. He knew Bernardi would tell him what was wrong.

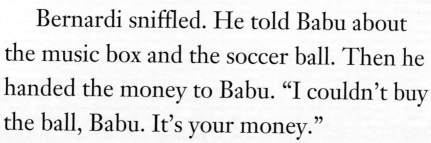

Bernardi sniffled. He told Babu about the music box and the soccer ball. Then he handed the money to Babu. "I couldn't buy the ball, Babu. It's your money."

Babu patted Bernardi's head. Then he placed the money in Bernardi's hand and held it, to show him that the money belonged to both of them.

Bernardi hung his head. "I don't want the ball anymore." He held out the money. "Take it, Babu. You decide what to do with the money."

Babu took the money and looked thoughtfully at Bernardi for a long time. Then he broke into a smile, signaled to Bernardi to wait, and walked out the door.

Bernardi sat quietly in the room as he waited for Babu. He wished he still had the music box. How could he have sold it?

Bernardi was sitting in the lamplight when Babu returned holding a paper bag. Babu pulled out a package and handed it to Bernardi.

Bernardi choked back a sob. He untied the string and pulled back the brown paper. His eyes opened wide when he saw what was inside. It was a school uniform!

Bernardi looked at Babu. "You paid for me to go to school?"

Babu nodded. Bernardi jumped up and hugged his grandfather.

FCAT Plot

Describe how Bernardi feels about Babu. Use information from the story in your answer.

While Bernardi held the new uniform to his chest, Babu went back outside. He returned holding something behind his back. With a flourish Babu held out a soccer ball made from string and Mama Valentina's gunnysack.

Bernardi put down his uniform and held the ball. He bounced it on one knee and it felt like the real thing.

"Thank you, Babu. It's wonderful!" Bernardi said to his grandfather and gave him a hug. Babu beamed. Bernardi decided that the ball was even better than the real thing.

Babu pulled one more surprise from the paper bag. It was an empty lard tin. As Babu began to make another music box, Bernardi put the water on the stove to boil. Then Bernardi hummed Babu's song as they sat in the lamplight and waited for their tea.

Exploring People and Places with Stephanie and Aaron

STEPHANIE STUVE-BODEEN once lived in a village in Tanzania, Africa. Tanzania is where this story takes place. While she was there, Stephanie lived near a school. It was like the one Bernardi wants to go to.

AARON BOYD knew he wanted to be an illustrator when he was just six years old. He would go to the library and study all the picture books. "I liked trying to read the story through just the pictures," he says. "It seemed very magical to me, making a story with pictures."

Other books illustrated by Aaron Boyd

 LOG ON Find out more about Stephanie Stuve-Bodeen and Aaron Boyd at **www.macmillanmh.com**

FCAT Author's Purpose

The author tells a story about a soccer ball that is special to a boy. Write a description of something that is special to you.

440

FCAT Comprehension Check

Retell the Story

Use the Retelling Cards
to retell the story.

Retelling Cards

Think and Compare

1. How does the setting of the
story help you understand
Bernardi and Babu? Use
details and information from
the story to support your
answer. **Reread: Plot**

Characters	Setting

2. Reread page 422. Why doesn't Bernardi
hum as he walks home after visiting the
vendors? **Analyze**

3. How is Bernardi's life like yours? How is it
different? Explain. **Evaluate**

4. Why do you think Bernardi feels sad when
he can't go to school? **Analyze**

5. Compare Bernardi's life with his
grandfather to Aki's and her
grandmother's in "E-mails from
Other Places" on pages 410–411.
Reading/Writing Across Texts

Genre

A Nonfiction Article gives information and facts about a topic.

Text Feature

Maps show where places are located.

Content Vocabulary

climate

capital

democracy

Where in the World Is Tanzania?

by Jeff Mateo

Africa is the second largest continent. It is so big that the United States could fit in it three times! Africa is between the Atlantic and Indian Oceans. It is south of the Mediterranean Sea. Africa has the hottest **climate** on Earth. This means the weather is hotter there than on any other continent.

There are 53 countries in Africa. Tanzania is a country in southeast Africa. Dodoma is its **capital** city. This is where the government is found. It is a **democracy**. This means that the people can vote for their leaders.

Tanzania has three types of land. The coastal area is long and flat. It is found along the Indian Ocean.

The plateau is large and flat. It is found in the middle of the country. It is covered in trees and tall grasses. A large part of it is the Great Rift Valley.

The mountains are in the west. The highest point is on Mount Kilimanjaro, which stands more than 19,000 feet tall.

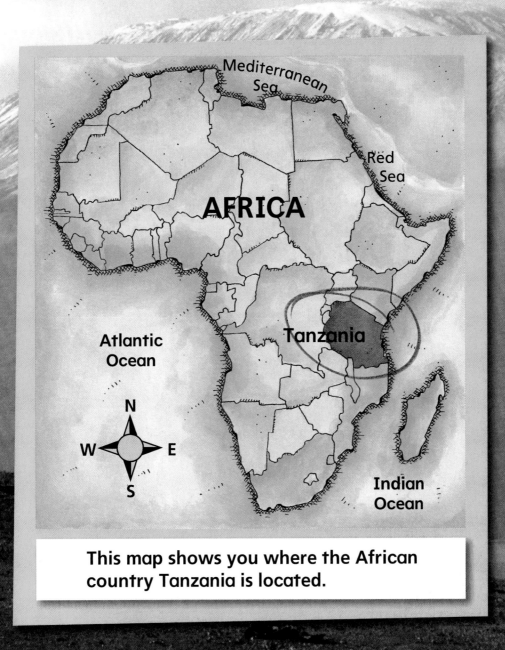

This map shows you where the African country Tanzania is located.

More than 33 million people live in Tanzania. There are 120 different tribes of people and each has its own customs and beliefs. The national language is Kiswahili. Tanzanians may speak English as well as the languages of their tribes.

Each tribe, such as the Makonde and Masai, has its own traditions and dances. Visitors come to learn about the people and watch the dances. The dances tell exciting stories.

Many people in Tanzania are farmers and miners. They dig minerals and gems, such as gold and diamonds, out of the ground.

Other Tanzanians help the tourists who come to visit the country. They work in hotels and give tours. Some Tanzanians make and sell crafts to tourists. Tourism is a big business in Tanzania. People come from all over the world to see the amazing wildlife.

Tanzania has many wild animals, such as lions, zebras, giraffes, and baboons. Many live in national parks, which are animal sanctuaries. The workers help protect the animals and the places where they live.

FCAT Connect and Compare

1. Which ocean is next to Tanzania? **Map**

2. Think about this article and *Babu's Song*. What new information does the article give you about Bernardi's life in Tanzania? **Reading/Writing Across Texts**

Social Studies Activity

Research another country in Africa. Find it on a map. Write a short report about it.

 Find out more about Africa at **www.macmillanmh.com**

FCAT Writer's Craft

Transitions
Good writers use transitions between paragraphs to make their writing flow smoothly.

Write About a Fun Trip

My transition connects my paragraphs.

My paragraphs vary, but the topic does not.

April 14

Today we took the best class trip ever! We went to the zoo and spent the whole day with different zookeepers. We watched the keepers freeze apples in giant blocks of ice as treats for the huge polar bears. We were also allowed to look inside the rooms where the animals spend the night. That was a surprise. I thought the zoo animals lived outside all of the time.

I had the greatest time. Maybe I'll be a zookeeper when I grow up!

Writing Prompt

A fun trip could be to somewhere close or to somewhere far away.

Think about a fun trip that you have taken. What made it fun?

Write about this fun trip.

 FCAT Writer's Checklist

 Focus: My writing is clearly about a fun trip.

 Organization: My writing includes paragraphs with transitions.

✓ **Support:** I include details that describe why the trip was fun.

 Conventions: My sentences are complete and punctuated correctly.

447

FCAT

Review

Author's Purpose
Compare and Contrast
Problem and Solution
Captions
Time Line
Homophones

Rico's ZEBRA

"We're going to use the art materials to make the animals we read about today," Mrs. Baxter told the children. "I want each of you to pick an animal you like," Mrs. Baxter said. "You can use any art materials you want."

There were many good artists in Rico's class, but Rico didn't think he was one of them. "Maybe I'll watch how the good artists make animals. Maybe that will help me."

He watched Jen drawing an elephant with a marker. Her lines were dark and strong. Her elephant looked great. Rico tried drawing a zebra the same way. But his lines came out too thick and bent.

Next, Rico walked to Sam's table. Sam was painting a peacock. But when Rico tried to paint the way Sam did, the paint splattered, turning his zebra into a muddy mess.

Next to Sam, Rico saw Anna working on a clay crocodile. It had big teeth and a long tail. "I like to work with clay. That's my way," she told Rico.

"Maybe I should stop trying to do what other kids do," Rico thought. He got cardboard, colored paper, and glue. He began to work on a zebra model.

"Cool zebra!" said Jen when Rico finished it. "Your model doesn't look like anyone else's!"

Everyone loved Rico's zebra.

"I guess I can be a good artist," Rico said to Mrs. Baxter. "I just have to work my own way."

THE MOTHER OF THE BABY BACKPACK

African mothers carry their babies everywhere they go.

Have you ever seen a baby carrier? A baby carrier is like a backpack for carrying a baby. Ann Moore introduced the idea of a baby carrier to American people.

Ann was a nurse in Africa in the early 1960s. She saw babies cradled in bright cloth wraps tied to their mothers' backs. This way, the mothers' hands were free to do other things.

In 1964, Ann had her own baby. She tried making a carrier like the one African mothers used. The carrier was like a backpack. Everywhere Ann went with her baby in the carrier, people asked, "Where can I buy one?"

early 1960s	1964	1965
Ann Moore is a nurse in Africa.	Ann has a baby.	Ann sells handmade carriers.

450

In 1965, Ann and her mother started selling handmade carriers. When the baby carrier appeared in a catalog, many people wanted it.

Ann received a patent for the baby carrier in 1969. By that time, the baby carrier had leg holes and straps that could be made longer or shorter. It could also be worn on the back or front.

By 1979, the baby carriers were made in a factory. More than 25,000 were sold every month. In 1985, Ann sold the company.

Now all over the world babies ride in baby carriers, safe and happy, close to their parents.

Ann Moore's baby carriers were very useful to parents.

Moms and dads give Moore's baby carrier a hand!

1969	1979	1985
Ann patents her baby carrier.	Baby carriers are made in factories.	Ann sells her company.

Glossary

What is a Glossary?

A glossary can help you find the **meanings** of words. If you see a word that you don't know, try to find it in the glossary. The words are in **alphabetical order**. **Guide words** at the top of each page tell you the first and last words on the page.

A **definition** is given for each word. An **example** shows the word used in a sentence. Each word is divided into **syllables**. Finally, the **part of speech** is given.

Sample Entry

Definition

Main entry — **burrow**   A hole dug in the ground by an animal. *A gopher lives in an* — Example sentence
underground **burrow**.

Syllable division — **bur•row** *noun.* — Part of Speech

453

Aa

adapted Made or became used to. *When he moved to Alaska, he* **adapted** *to the cold weather.*
a·dapt·ed *verb.* Past tense of **adapt**.

agreed To have thought or felt the same way as someone else. *My friends all* **agreed** *it was a good book.*
a·greed *verb.* Past tense of **agree**.

allowed Let someone do something. *David* **allowed** *Jen to use his camera.*
al·lowed *verb.* Past tense of **allow**.

appeal To be attractive or interesting. *Does playing a board game* **appeal** *to you now?*
ap·peal *verb.*

areas Spaces or sections that are part of a larger place. *We took a trip to the wooded* **areas** *of Maine.*
ar·e·as *plural noun.* Plural of **area**.

aroma A pleasant or agreeable smell. *The flowers gave off a wonderful* **aroma**.
a·ro·ma *noun.*

assembled   Brought or gathered together. *A crowd assembled for the concert.*
as·sem·bled *verb.* Past tense of **assemble**.

author   A person who has written a book, story, play, article, or poem. *Peggy Rathmann is the author of Officer Buckle and Gloria.*
au·thor *noun.*

Bb

balance   A safe position where something can't roll away or fall off. *I lost my balance while skiing and fell.*
bal·ance *noun.*

beasts   Any animals that have four feet. *The zoo is home to beasts like giraffes and lions.*
beasts *plural noun.* Plural of **beast**.

beloved   Loved very much. *The class pet was beloved by all the students.*
be·lov·ed *adjective.*

beware   To be on one's guard; be careful. *Beware of speeding cars when crossing the street.*
be·ware *verb.*

beyond   Farther on. *Look beyond the desert and you'll see the mountains.*
be·yond *preposition, adverb.*

blooming Having flowers. *The rose bushes will be **blooming** in June.*

bloom·ing *adjective.*

burrow A hole dug in the ground by an animal. *A gopher lives in an underground **burrow**.*

bur·row *noun.*

Cc

capital A city where leaders of a country or state work. *Washington, D.C. is the **capital** of the United States of America.*

cap·i·tal *noun.*

climate The usual weather conditions of a place or region throughout the year. *The desert's **climate** is much warmer than the tundra's climate.*

cli·mate *noun.*

collection A group of things gathered together. *The museum has the world's largest **collection** of dinosaur fossils.*

col·lec·tion *noun.*

concern Serious interest. *We were full of **concern** for our teacher who was out sick for a whole week.*

con·cern *noun.*

conservation The wise use of the forests, rivers, minerals, and other natural resources of a country. *Water **conservation** is an important issue in many countries.*

con·ser·va·tion *noun.*

creating Causing something to be or happen. *The children were* **creating** *new paintings during art class.*

cre·at·ing *verb.* Inflected form of **create**.

Dd

democracy A government that is run by the people who live under it. *The United States is a* **democracy***.*

dem·o·cra·cy *noun.*

deserted Not lived in or on. *The sailor was shipwrecked on a* **deserted** *island.*

des·ert·ed *adjective.*

design A drawing or outline used as a guide or pattern. *The architect's* **design** *for the museum was beautiful.*

de·sign *noun.*

destroy To ruin completely. *A hurricane can* **destroy** *a building.*

de·stroy *verb.*

devoured Ate or consumed. *The hungry teenager* **devoured** *the sandwiches.*

de·vour·ed *verb.* Past tense of **devour**.

directions Information or steps to follow about how to do something. *Follow the* **directions** *on the package to bake the muffins.*

di·rec·tions *plural noun.* Plural of **direction**.

discovered To have seen or found out for the first time. Alexander *discovered* a rabbit hole in the backyard yesterday.

dis·cov·ered *verb.* Past tense of **discover**.

distant Far away in distance or time; not near. *Some of our distant relatives live in Australia.*

dis·tant *adjective.*

Ee

endangered In danger of dying out. *Pandas in China are an endangered species.*

en·dan·gered *adjective.*

events Things that happen, especially things that are important to people. *I like to read about current events in the newspaper.*

e·vents *plural noun.* Plural of **event**.

exclaimed Spoken or shouted suddenly with strong feelings. *"I just won the game," Christopher exclaimed.*

ex·claimed *verb.* Past tense of **exclaim**.

extinct When a thing dies out and no more of its kind are living anywhere on Earth. *Dinosaurs are extinct.*

ex·tinct *adjective.*

Ff

familiar Known because of having been heard or seen before. *The actor on television looked **familiar**.*

fa·mi·liar *adjective.*

fetch To go after and bring back; get. *Please **fetch** two more plates from the kitchen.*

fetch *verb.*

figure A form, outline, or shape. *Each **figure** on the shelf is part of Mom's collection of bells.*

fig·ure *noun.*

footprint A mark made by a foot or shoe. *I left behind a **footprint** when I walked through the wet sand.*

foot·print *noun.*

forgetting Not being able to remember something. *Diego kept **forgetting** to bring his pet in for show-and-tell.*

for·get·ting *verb.* Inflected form of **forget**.

freezes   Becomes solid from cold. *Water that* **freezes** *turns into ice.*
free·zes *verb.* Present tense of **freeze**.

Gg

gas   A substance that spreads to fill a space. *Air is a kind of* **gas.**
gas *noun.*

gathered   Brought together. *Carol* **gathered** *her favorite books to read on vacation.*
gath·ered *verb.* Past tense of **gather**.

glamorous   Interesting, exciting, and charming. *The actor went to many* **glamorous** *parties.*
glam·or·ous *adjective.*

glanced   Took a quick look. *The driver* **glanced** *behind her before safely changing lanes.*
glanced *verb.* Past tense of **glance**.

gleamed   Glowed or shone. *The new bike* **gleamed** *in the sunlight.*
gleamed *verb.* Past tense of **gleam**.

goalie   The player who defends the goal in soccer, hockey, and some other sports. *Our* **goalie** *made a great save at the end of the game.*
goal·ie *noun.*

grasslands Lands covered mainly with grass, where animals feed. *Scientists are trying to protect U.S. grasslands.*
grass·lands *plural noun.* Plural of **grassland**.

Hh

handy Within reach. *Dad keeps his car keys handy in his front pocket.*
hand·y *adjective.*

hardest Needing or using a lot of work. *My hardest chore is cleaning out the garage each year.*
har·dest *adjective.* Superlative of **hard**.

Ii

imagination Pictures in a person's mind that are not real. *Ernesto used his imagination to create a new ending to the story.*
i·mag·i·na·tion *noun.*

imagine To picture a person or thing in the mind. *Try to imagine what cars will look like in the year 2050.*
i·mag·ine *verb.*

immense Of great size; very large. *Redwood trees can be immense, measuring more than 22 feet wide.*
im·mense *adjective.*

impossible Not able to happen or be done. *The snowstorm made it **impossible** to get to school today.*
im·pos·si·ble *adjective.*

information Knowledge about something. *Where can I get **information** about crocodiles?*
in·for·ma·tion *noun.*

instrument **1.** A tool that helps a person do something. *The dentist used an **instrument** to scrape my teeth.* **2.** Something used to make music. *Which musical **instrument** do you play?*
in·stru·ment *noun.*

interviewed To have asked questions to get information. *I **interviewed** the principal for the school newspaper.*
in·ter·viewed *verb.* Past tense of **interview.**

invent To make or think of something for the first time. *It took Thomas Edison a long time to **invent** the lightbulb.*
in·vent *verb.*

itches Tickling or stinging feelings in the skin. *Kim rubbed her back to scratch her **itches**.*
itch·es *plural noun.* Plural of **itch.**

Jj

jabbing Poking with something pointed. *Jason moved his books so they weren't* **jabbing** *into his side.*

jab·bing *verb.* Inflected form of **jab**.

Ll

lengthy Being very long in distance or time. *The kangaroo made* **lengthy** *leaps to cross the field quickly.*

length·y *adjective.*

liquids Materials that are wet and flow. *Water and juice are examples of* **liquids.**

liquids *plural noun.* Plural of **liquid**.

lunar Having to do with the moon. *My brother and I like to read about the astronauts'* **lunar** *landings.*

lu·nar *adjective.*

Mm

memories Persons or things remembered from the past. *My favorite* **memories** *from camp are playing soccer and swimming.*

mem·o·ries *plural noun.* Plural of **memory**.

menu A list of food offered in a restaurant. *Patricia likes to read the whole* **menu** *before choosing what to eat.*

men·u *noun.*

muscles Bundles of tissue that move certain parts of the body. *My aunt goes to the gym every day to keep her* **muscles** *strong.*

mu·scles *plural noun.* Plural of **muscle**.

Nn

nibble To eat quickly and with small bites. *A mouse will **nibble** cheese.*
nib·ble *verb.*

noble Impressive looking. *The **noble** lion stood proudly at the opening to the cave.*
no·ble *adjective.*

nocturnal Being seen or happening at night. *Bats are **nocturnal** animals.*
noc·tur·nal *adjective.*

Oo

occasions Important or special events. *Holidays are important **occasions** for my family.*
oc·ca·sions *plural noun.* Plural of **occasion**.

oceans Very large bodies of salt water. *It is possible to travel around the world by sailing over the **oceans**.*
o·ceans *plural noun.* Plural of **ocean**.

Pp

planet   A huge object that travels around the sun. *Earth is a **planet** in our solar system.*
plan·et *noun.*

pleasant   In a nice or friendly way. *The cab driver was **pleasant** to all his riders.*
pleas·ant *adjective.*

pollution   Waste that harms land, water, or air. *People are trying to clean up the **pollution** in our oceans and rivers.*
pol·lu·tion *noun.*

pottery   Things made from baked clay. *Our art teacher makes beautiful **pottery** bowls.*
pot·ter·y *noun.*

powerful   Having great power and importance. *The president is a **powerful** member of government.*
pow·er·ful *adjective.*

predict   To use what you know to tell what will happen. *Scientists try to **predict** when an earthquake will happen.*
pre·dict *verb.*

preen   To make oneself smooth or sleek. *Birds **preen** by washing and smoothing their feathers.*
preen *verb.*

prevent   To keep something from happening. *A seatbelt will help **prevent** an injury in a car accident.*
prevent *verb.*

prickly   Having small, sharp thorns or points. *The cactus plants are **prickly**.*
prick·ly *adjective.*

products   Things that are made or created. *The cans of food you buy in stores are **products**.*
prod·ucts *plural noun.* Plural of **product**.

promised   Said that something will or will not happen. *I **promised** that I would clean my room.*
prom·ised *verb.* Past tense of **promise**.

protected   Guarded from danger or harm. *Florida laws have **protected** manatees.*
pro·tect·ed *verb.* Past tense of **protect**.

puddles   Small shallow pools of water or other liquids. *Our driveway has many **puddles** after a storm.*
pud·dles *plural noun.* Plural of **puddle**.

Rr

randomly Made or done by chance, with no clear pattern. *The teacher **randomly** called three students to the front of the room.*
ran·dom·ly *adverb.*

ranger's Belonging to a person whose job it is to protect a forest. *We used the **ranger's** truck to get to our campsite.*
ran·ger's *possessive singular noun.* Possessive of **ranger**.

remains Things that are left. *The explorers found the **remains** of an ancient building.*
re·mains *plural noun.*

Ss

saddest The most unhappy. *Of my friends, I was the **saddest** when our teacher moved away.*
sad·dest *adjective.* Superlative of **sad**.

sanctuary A natural area where animals are kept safe. *The animals in the **sanctuary** are safe from hunters.*
sanc·tu·a·ry *noun.*

scent A smell. *The **scent** of roses filled the air.*
scent *noun.*

signal A way of showing people to do something. *A red traffic light is a **signal** to stop.*
sig·nal *noun.*

simmered Cooked at or just below the boiling point. *The soup **simmered** on the stove all day.*
sim·mered *verb.* Past tense of **simmer**.

soil The dirt on the surface of the earth. *We dig in **soil** to plant flowers.*

soil *noun.*

solids Firm materials with definite shape. *Rocks are examples of **solids.***

solids *plural noun.*

spacecraft A vehicle used for flight in outer space. *Astronauts used **spacecraft** to explore the moon.*

space·craft *noun.*

surface The outside of a thing. *The **surface** of the road is bumpy.*

sur·face *noun.*

Tt

talent A natural ability or skill. *Clara has a **talent** for drawing realistic pictures.*

tal·ent *noun.*

temperature A measure of how hot or cold something is. *You can find the **temperature** by using a thermometer.*

tem·per·a·ture *noun.*

trade The giving of one thing in return for something else. *Swapping an apple for an orange is a fair **trade**.*

trade *noun.*

treasures Money, jewels, or things that are worth a lot or have meaning. *Scientists discovered **treasures** in the ancient tomb.*

treas·ures *plural noun.* Plural of **treasure**.

trouble A difficult or dangerous condition. *We'll be in a lot of* **trouble** *if we don't complete the assignment.*
trou·ble *noun.*

Uu

uprooted Torn or pulled up by the roots. *A bulldozer* **uprooted** *trees and bushes.*
up·rooted *verb.* Past tense of **uproot**.

Vv

vast Very great in size. *Our tiny ship sailed across the* **vast** *sea.*
vast *adjective.*

vendors People who sell things. *The fruit* **vendors** *were selling apples, bananas, and oranges.*
ven·dors *plural noun.* Plural of **vendor**.

violent Happening with or because of a strong force. *The* **violent** *earthquake destroyed many homes.*
vi·o·lent *adjective.*

visible   Able to be seen. *My house is **visible** from the street.*
vis·i·ble *adjective.*

voyage   A long trip by water, over land, or through space. *An ocean **voyage** can take more than a week.*
voy·age *noun.*

Ww

warning   Notice about a danger. *The sign was a **warning** that the road curved sharply ahead.*
warn·ing *noun.*

watch   **1.** To look at something or someone carefully. *Leslie likes to **watch** her baby brother play with his toys.* **2.** A small clock worn on a person's wrist. *Carlos checked his **watch** to make sure he wasn't late for practice.*
watch *verb.*
watch *noun.*

wider   Covering a larger area from side to side. *Some aisles in the supermarket are **wider** than others.*
wi·der *adjective.* Comparative of **wide**.

wiggled   Moved from side to side in short, sudden movements. *I **wiggled** my loose tooth.*
wig·gled *verb.* Past tense of **wiggle**.

Acknowledgments

The publisher gratefully acknowledges permission to reprint the following copyrighted materials:

Babu's Song by Stephanie Stuve-Bodeen, illustrated by Aaron Boyd. Text copyright © 2003 by Stephanie Stuve-Bodeen. Illustrations copyright © 2003 by Aaron Boyd. Reprinted by permission of Lee & Low Books, Inc.

"Bella Had a New Umbrella" by Eve Merriam from BLACKBERRY INK. Text copyright © 1985 by Eve Merriam. Reprinted with permission of William Morrow.

"Brush Dance" from POCKET POEMS by Robin Bernard. Text copyright © 2004 by Robin Bernard. Reprinted by permission of Penguin Putnam Books for Young Readers.

"Crayons" from READ-ALOUD RHYMES FOR THE VERY YOUNG by Marchette Chute. Text copyright © 1974 by Marchette Chute. Reprinted by permission of Random House, Inc.

"Dig Wait Listen: A Desert Toad's Tale" by April Pulley Sayre, illustrated by Barbara Bash. Text copyright © 2001 by April Pulley Sayre. Illustrations copyright © 2001 by Barbara Bash. Reprinted by permission of HarperCollins Publishers.

"Goose's Story" by Cari Best, illustrated by Holly Meade. Text copyright © 2002 by Cari Best. Illustrations copyright © 2002 by Holly Meade. Reprinted by permission of Farrar, Straus and Giroux.

"It Fell in the City" from BLACKBERRY INK by Eve Merriam. Text copyright © 1985 by Eve Merriam. Reprinted by permission of William Morrow and Company.

"Mice and Beans" by Pam Muñoz Ryan, illustrated by Joe Cepeda. Text copyright © 2001 by Pam Muñoz Ryan. Illustrations copyright © 2001 by Joe Cepeda. Reprinted by permission of Scholastic Press, a division of Scholastic Inc.

"The Moon" by Seymour Simon. Text copyright © 1984, 2003 by Seymour Simon. Reprinted by permission of Simon & Schuster Children's Publishing Division.

"Night Comes" from READ-ALOUD RHYMES FOR THE VERY YOUNG by Beatrice Schenk de Regniers. Copyright © 1977 by Beatrice Schenk de Regniers. Reprinted by permission of Houghton Mifflin.

"Nutik, the Wolf Pup" by Jean Craighead George, illustrated by Ted Rand. Text copyright © 2001 by Julie Productions, Inc. Illustrations copyright © 2001 by Ted Rand. Reprinted with permission from HarperCollins Publishers.

"Pushing Up The Sky" from PUSHING UP THE SKY by Joseph Bruchac. Text copyright © 2000 by Joseph Bruchac. Reprinted by permission of Penguin Putnam Books for Young Readers.

"Splish! Splash! Animal Baths" by April Pulley Sayre. Copyright © 2000 by April Pulley Sayre. Reprinted by permission of The Millbrook Press, Inc.

"Super Storms" by Seymour Simon. Text copyright © 2002 by Seymour Simon. Reprinted by permission of SeaStar Books, a division of North-South Books, Inc.

"The Ugly Vegetables" by Grace Lin. Text and illustrations copyright © 1999 by Grace Lin. Reprinted by permission of Charlesbridge Publishing.

BOOK COVERS

AMELIA AND ELEANOR GO FOR A RIDE. Reprinted by permission of Scholastic, Inc. ARMY ANT PARADE. Reprinted by permission of Henry Holt and Company, LLC. CAPTAIN BOB TAKES FLIGHT. Reprinted by permission of Simon & Schuster Children's Publishing Division. COUNT YOUR WAY THROUGH AFRICA. Reprinted by permission of Carolrhoda Books, Inc. DESERT GIANT: THE WORLD OF SAGUARO CACTUS. Reprinted by permission of Sierra Club Books for Children. DESTINATION MARS. Reprinted by permission of HarperCollins Publishers. FORTUNE COOKIE FORTUNES. Reprinted by permission of Random House, Inc. GET ON BOARD: THE STORY OF THE UNDERGROUND RAILROAD. Reprinted by permission of Scholastic Inc. GORILLAS. Reprinted by permission of HarperCollins Publishers. HELLO OCEAN. Reprinted by permission of Charlesbridge Publishing. I CAN'T TAKE A BATH. Reprinted by permission of Scholastic Inc. IN THE HEART OF THE VILLAGE: THE WORLD OF THE INDIAN BANYAN TREE. Reprinted by permission of Sierra Club Books for Children. JANNA AND THE KINGS. Reprinted by permission of Lee & Low Books, Inc. KOI AND THE KOLA NUTS. Reprinted by permission of Simon & Schuster Children's Publishing Division. MARS. Reprinted by permission of William Morrow and Company, Inc. NOODLE MAN: THE PASTA SUPERHERO. Reprinted by permission of Scholastic Inc. NUTIK & AMAROQ PLAY BALL. Reprinted by permission of HarperCollins Publishers. OKIE-DOKIE ARTICHOKIES. Reprinted by permission of Penguin Putnam Books for Young Readers. ONE HUNDRED IS A FAMILY. Reprinted by permission of Hyperion Books for Children. PLANETS AROUND THE SUN. Reprinted by permission of North-South Books Inc. SHRINKING VIOLET. Reprinted by permission of Farrar, Straus and Giroux. THE FIRST STRAWBERRIES: A CHEROKEE STORY. Reprinted by permission of Penguin Putnam Books for Young Readers. THIRTEEN MOONS ON TURTLE'S BACK: A NATIVE AMERICAN YEAR OF MOONS. Reprinted by permission of Penguin Putnam Books for Young Readers. THREE CHEERS FOR CATHERINE THE GREAT! Reprinted by permission of DK Publishing, Inc.

ILLUSTRATIONS
Cover Illustration: Gary Overacre

38: Rex Barron. 46-73: Holly Meade. 72: (bc) Giselle Potter. (bcr) Giselle Potter. 76: Joe Lemonnier. 128-149: Ted Rand. 148: (bcr) Wendell Minor. 155: Daniel Del Valle. 156-157: Karen Dugan. 164-187: Barbara Bash. 196-197: Laura Ovresat. 198-213: Stephano Vitale. 234-257: Grace Lin. 290-291: Kristin Barr. 294-295: Keiko Motoyama. 297: Greg Harris. 300-301: Bernard Adnet. 302-333: Joe Cepeda. 346: (tr) Beth G. Johnson. 364: Daniel Del Valle. 382-398: Eric Velasquez. 403-405: Eric Velasquez. 405: (bkgd) Wetzel and Company. 410-411: Rob Schuster. 412-441: Aaron Boyd. 448-449: Deborah Melmon. 452-453: Joy Allen.

PHOTOGRAPHY
All photographs are by Macmillan McGraw-Hill (MMH) except as noted below.

10-11: MedioImages/SuperStock. 12-13: (bkgd) Lee Cates/Getty Images, Inc. 13: (tr) Craig Tuttle/CORBIS. 14-15: Courtesy of Peter Arnold, Inc. Wildlife Pictures. 16-17: Peter Weimann/Animals Animals. 18-19: Ralph Reinhold/Animals Animals. 20: (bl) Gerard Lacz/Animals Animals. 20-21: (t) Minden Pictures/Tim Fitzharris. 22: Minden Pictures/Frans Lanting. 23: Robert Winslow/Animals Animals. 24-25: The Nation Audubon Society Collection/Photo Researchers/Mitch Reardon. 26-27: Peter Arnold/Gunter Ziesler. 28: Minden Pictures/ Frans Lanting. 29: The National Audubon Society Collection/Photo Researchers/ Gregory Ochocki. 30-31: The National Audubon Society/Photo Researchers Allan Power. 32-33: Mike Severns/Getty Images. 34: The National Audubon Society/Photo Researchers/Mark Phillips. 35: Minden Pictures/Frans Lanting. 36: (l) Frans Lanting/Minden Pictures; (tr) courtesy of April Pulley Sayre. 37: Peter Weimann/Animals Animals/Earth Scenes. 40: Ross Whitaker/The Image Bank/Getty Images, Inc. 41: Tim Davis/Stone/Getty Images, Inc. 42-43: JEFFREY L. ROTMAN/Getty Images. 44: (bl) Darrell Gulin/CORBIS. 44-45: (bkgd) Chase Swift/CORBIS. 72: (tr) courtesy of Farrar, Straus & Giroux; (cl) courtesy of Holly Meade; Daniel J. Cox/Stone/Getty Images, Inc. 76: Dale Shields, the "Pelican Man." 77: Diego Lezama Orezzoli/CORBIS. 78: Photodisc Green/Getty Images, Inc. 79: Kim Steele/Getty Images, Inc. 80-81: Barbara Stitzer/Photo Edit Inc. 82: (tr) Gloria H. Chomica/ Masterfile; (br) Judy Griesedieck; (b) Jim Brandenburg/Minden Pictures. 83: ZSSD/Minden Pictures. 84-85: (b) CORBIS. 85: (tr) Walter Bibikow/The Image Bank/Getty Images, Inc.; (cr) Felicia Martinez/ Photo Edit Inc.; (br) Photodisc/Getty Images, Inc. 86: (tl) Comstock Images/Alamy; (tcl) Karl Weatherly/CORBIS; (bcl) Mark Gibson/Index Stock Imagery; (bl) Hank Morgan/Photo Researchers, Inc. 86-87: (br) Courtesy Landscape Structures Inc. 87: Arthur Tilley/Taxi/Getty Images. 88: Marko Kokic/IFRC. 90: Ryan McVay/Photodisc/Getty Images. 91: (c) Dian Lofton for TFK; (cr) Photolink/Getty Images, Inc.;